BUSINESS ETHICS

AND

ETHICAL BUSINESS

Robert Audi
University of Notre Dame

New York   Oxford
OXFORD UNIVERSITY PRESS
2009

Oxford University Press, Inc., publishes works that further Oxford University's
objective of excellence in research, scholarship, and education.

Oxford   New York
Auckland   Cape Town   Dar es Salaam   Hong Kong   Karachi
Kuala Lumpur   Madrid   Melbourne   Mexico City   Nairobi
New Delhi   Shanghai   Taipei   Toronto

With offices in
Argentina   Austria   Brazil   Chile   Czech Republic   France   Greece
Guatemala   Hungary   Italy   Japan   Poland   Portugal   Singapore
South Korea   Switzerland   Thailand   Turkey   Ukraine   Vietnam

Copyright © 2009 by Oxford University Press, Inc.

Published by Oxford University Press, Inc.
198 Madison Avenue, New York, New York 10016
www.oup.com

Library of Congress Cataloging-in-Publication Data
Audi, Robert, 1941–
　Business ethics and ethical business / Robert Audi.
　　p.　cm.
　Includes bibliographical references and index.
　ISBN-13: 978-0-19-536910-6 (pbk.)
　ISBN-13: 978-0-19-536911-3 (hardcover)
　1. Business ethics.　2. Social responsibility of business.　3. Corporations—
Environmental aspects.　4. Corporations—Moral and ethical aspects.
　5. International business enterprises—Moral and ethical aspects.
　6. Globalization—Moral and ethical aspects.　I. Title.

HF5387.A825 2009
174'.4—dc22   2008018825

Printing number: 9 8 7 6 5 4 3 2 1

Printed in the United States of America
on acid-free paper

To the Memory of my Brother
Alfred J. Audi
Consummate Entrepreneur

CONTENTS

v

PART III
ETHICAL PROBLEMS OF GLOBAL BUSINESS

PREFACE

This book is an analytical presentation of major problems in business ethics in the light of major ethical standards. The problems range from the place of business in society to the ethics of internal management to challenges of international business. The ethical standards are mainly the universally respected principles and values that are common not only to major ethical approaches, but also to many of the world's religions. These include justice and veracity, beneficence and loyalty, and freedom and respect for persons.

A distinctive element in the book is the way it anchors the two main competing views of business in society—the free market view and the corporate social responsibility (CSR) approach—in two major competing political traditions that are each important for understanding democracy. Another element is its integration of major ethical theories with the analysis of common problems in business ethics. The theories run from Aristotelian virtue ethics to the rule-based ethics of Immanuel Kant, the utilitarianism represented by John Stuart Mill, and the common-sense ethics associated with W. D. Ross's intuitionism, whose roots go back at least to Aquinas.

The book is also distinctive in providing a large number of brief concept definitions important in business ethics. The concepts include *affirmative action, bribery, conflict of interest, intellectual property, risk, stakeholders, sustainability, technology transfer, transparency*, and *value*. Many definitions are recapitulated in the Glossary. Still another distinctive element is the treatment of *rights*: their nature is clarified and their importance stressed, but their limitations as only one focus in ethics are also shown. The relation between law and ethics is a further concern in business ethics. Several parts of the book explore it. The result is a presentation of business ethics that enables readers new to the field to acquire the basic conceptual and ethical tools needed to address moral problems facing business in a pluralistic democracy.

I have been guided by the sense of a need for a brief, conceptually sophisticated but non-technical book that can be read in either short or long courses and in whole or in part. Each chapter is largely self-contained. The book should be especially useful for modules or in courses that pursue case studies in detail. It contains enough ethical analysis and explanation of basic ethics to free instructors from having to assign lengthy or difficult readings in general ethics. It is readily usable, however, with virtually any standard collection of readings in business ethics. If readings in general ethics are also included, the connections to them will be clear.

The book is also designed to free instructors who have limited time for teaching business ethics—say because they do it in an executive MBA, marketing, or management course—from needing a case book or compiling extensive case studies. The Appendix contains sixteen case scenarios modeled on ethical problems common in the business world. Many of the book's examples are also modeled on cases in which actual businesses have faced the ethical problems under discussion. Small, family-owned businesses, as well as large companies, are taken into account throughout. The concrete examples of ethical problems, like the individual chapters, are self-contained, but the examples and analyses can be developed in the light of case studies in the relevant problem area or specialized knowledge of the kind of business in question.

In arriving at short formulations of major ethical views, I have been greatly helped (perhaps emboldened) by previous work in ethics. My *Moral Knowledge and Ethical Character* (Oxford, 1997) explores many major views in ethics and outlines my own. A wide-ranging political theory with much discussion of the ethical foundations of democracy is developed in my *Religious Commitment and Secular Reason* (Cambridge, 2000). *The Good in the Right: A Theory of Intuition and Intrinsic Value* (Princeton, 2004) constructs and defends a common-sense ethical pluralism that forms the normative core of the decision model presented in Chapter 4. More recently, I have published a short accessible book that develops a theory of value and offers a comparative ethical perspective on major ethical challenges facing the contemporary world (*Moral Value and Human Diversity*, Oxford, 2007). Collectively, these books underlie many points in this one. The analysis they contain enables me to offer brief formulations knowing that readers who want explication or supporting arguments can turn to them or works they cite.

The book has a point of view and an underlying ethics, but it does not present these as the only plausible framework. Its aim is both to present problems and principles of business ethics and to enhance both the capacity and the motivation to make ethically sound decisions in business practice. It defends many ethical principles as apt for business ethics and makes many ethical assertions; but it also raises problems and questions that can be creatively explored in discussion. My hope is that those problems and questions will be widely pursued to the benefit of businesses themselves.

Acknowledgments

Comments from and discussions with my colleagues, Georges Enderle, Patrick Murphy, and Oliver Williams, C.S.C., have helped me greatly. Students in my undergraduate and MBA business ethics courses have also provided valuable reactions to early drafts. For other comments, often extensive and detailed, I am grateful to Joanne Ciulla, David DiQuattro, Robert Garcia, Bernard Gert, Jerry Goodstein, Peter Hadreas, Mitchell Haney, Mark Jensen, Nathan King, Peter Madsen, Alexei Marcoux, Kevin Mesiewicz, Kenny Moore, William Sauser, David Solomon, Richard Stone, and Elaine Weinstein. Responses and comments from anonymous readers and from many colleagues at the Mendoza College of Business at Notre Dame—Edward Conlon, Michael Crant,

Thomas Frecka, John Gaski, Timothy Gilbride, David Harvigsen, Jack Keane, Barry Keating, Ken Milani, Elizabeth Moore, William Nichols, Connie Porter, and, especially, Matt Bloom, Amy Colbert, Kevin Misiewicz, James O'Rourke, John Sherry, Lee Tavis, Ann Tenbrunsel, and Carolyn Woo—have been of great help. The advice of my editor, Robert Miller, has been invaluable at many points, and help from Marianne Paul, Project Editor, has been indispensible. I also want to acknowledge the great benefits of conversing with and reading many colleagues in business or applied ethics at other institutions, particularly Denis Arnold, Tom Beauchamp, John Boatright, George Brenkert, Marvin Brown, Thomas Carson, Gerald Cavanagh, David DeCosse, Richard DeGeorge, Joseph DesJardins, Thomas Donaldson, Kevin Gibson, Kenneth Goodpaster, Eugene Heath, Thomas Klein, Loren Lomasky, Ian Maitland, Douglas May, Rex Mixon, Denis Moberg, Jeffrey Moriarty, Lisa Newton, Scott Rae, Donald Robin, Jeffery Smith, the late Robert Solomon, Manuel Velasquez, Gary Weaver, Ben Wempe, Patricia Werhane, and especially, Norman Bowie, Edwin Hartman, and Kirk Hanson, Director of the Markkula Center for Applied Ethics at Santa Clara University where earlier versions of several chapters were presented. Finally, I am deeply grateful to the families of David E. Gallo and Joseph E. Gallo for their support of ethics at the Mendoza College of Business at Notre Dame. Without that support and the support of the College and its Department of Management, this book would never have been written.

PART I

The Role of Business
in a Free Democracy

1

TWO DEMOCRATIC TRADITIONS

Businesses do not operate in a social vacuum. They presuppose a social setting. This book will discuss business in the context of a free democracy existing in a global context. Free democracies are *free* in the sense that they protect liberty; they are *democratic* in their commitment to the standard of one person, one vote. Businesses cannot flourish without freedom. Just how *much* freedom they should have is a central question for business ethics. So is the question of what standard of equality businesses should respect in dealing with individuals. Moreover, granting that some inequality among persons is inevitable, how *much* inequality—in wealth and power, for instance—should free democracies allow economic freedom to create? Great wealth in a few people can give them highly disproportionate political power. Economic freedom, however, tends to result in great wealth on the part of some who have special skills or good fortune. There is controversy over how much economic freedom is needed for a democracy to flourish. Does governmental regulation of business reduce economic opportunity, or the average standard of living, or the quantity or quality of political participation? We should consider two major approaches to these questions. One gives priority to freedom, the other to a kind of equality.

Foundations of Capitalism

The Declaration of Independence cites "life, liberty and the pursuit of happiness" as "unalienable rights" of all. Positions close to this are standard in the constitutional thinking of modern democracies. Before the Founders of the United States signed this striking affirmation, the English philosopher John Locke affirmed similar rights: to "life, liberty and property."[1] Property is no guarantee of happiness. But for at least most of humanity, happiness is unattainable without some property, and free democracies—those whose governments are truly *of*, *by*, and *for* the people—always protect property rights.

Property is something *owned*. This implies a right to use it, give it, or—assuming economic freedom—sell it. Many thinkers take property rights to be a kind of moral right, belonging to us simply in virtue of our humanity. At least the majority of them are also legal rights, belonging to us under a legal system that protects them. Property rights with legal status are crucial for economic freedom and indeed, for capitalism, conceived as a social system in which free trade is widespread and legally protected. What we own we can trade; what we legally own we (normally) can legally trade.

Capitalism contrasts with socialism, which (in a pure form) is a system allowing little private property; "the people," through government, own manufacturing, agricultural lands, and everything else of major economic importance. Socialism need not exist in a pure form (and rarely if ever has), but a given segment of society, such as the healthcare system, can be socialized to one or another degree. A joke about capitalism, socialism, and totalitarian communism like that of Stalinist Russia captures part of the contrast. It starts with totalitarian communism: you have two cows; the government seizes them and shoots you— unless you agree to maintain and milk them as ordered. Socialism: you have two cows; the government takes them, but gives you some milk. Capitalism: you have two cows; you sell one and buy a bull.

Two Conceptions of Democracy

Property rights are clearly essential for economic vitality and for flourishing democracies. But there are two major democratic traditions that bear on how *far* property rights go and, correspondingly, on how much wealth an individual may acquire. They also imply much about the relation between business and government.

Both traditions, moreover, derive largely from ethical ideals: those of liberty and of a kind of basic equality among persons.

Locke took property rights to be essential for a just society. He also had a theory of property acquisition that provides a rationale for individuals' holding great wealth. It has influenced the establishment of property rights in the United States and elsewhere. He held that one can acquire unowned land (as he took unsettled America to be) by mixing one's labor with it, say farming it, so long as there is "as much and as good for others." By their labor the ancestors of some of us, then, could have ethically acquired hundreds of acres and amassed wealth. Since we can sell land—or its products—at a profit and pass wealth to our children without high inheritance tax, it is easy to see how huge fortunes can be acquired—and how people who come to a country too late may have to labor for others at whatever pay they can get.

On this Lockean view (a precursor of contemporary libertarianism), the role of government is to protect property from theft or invasion and to enforce contracts, not to control the economy or restrict free trade. The conception of free democracy we are considering tends to go with a *free market view* of the relation between government and business. On any plausible free market view, *some* limitations of economic freedom are justified. Without taxes, for instance, government, as distinct from private militias, is not feasible. If government is to go beyond policing and military functions, moreover, say by providing for public education, for basic public health, and for transportation, the tax rate must be higher. How high and how graduated it is to be are disputed in the free market tradition, as in others.

In contrast to the democratic tradition associated with Locke—sometimes called the tradition of English liberty—there is a quite different democratic perspective. It is strongly associated with the French philosopher Jean-Jacques Rousseau and sometimes called the tradition of French liberty.[2] The famous slogan of the French Revolution is not "life, liberty, and property" (central notions in the *Declaration of Independence*), but "liberty, equality, fraternity." The major contrast between the two traditions concerns equality. The difference is not over one person, one vote (which is central for any democracy), but over equality as something to be pursued. On the free market view, liberty implies the right to become *unequal* in wealth, political influence, and cultural importance—so long as one person, one vote is preserved and there is enough opportunity to allow everyone to compete fairly. By contrast, in the egalitarian tradition, although a degree of socioeconomic inequality is possible, prevention of huge inequalities is an aim of the system. This may be taken to support "fraternity," a kind of social harmony that is held to promote social cooperation and collective prosperity.

Another argument for the importance of limiting inequalities is that vast amounts of wealth threaten democracy by placing great political power in the hands of a few who can "buy" votes or bring economic pressure on some (such as legislators) to vote their way. Buying political ads can also be an instance of disproportionate political influence. Limitations on campaign contributions in the United States are in part a response to these and similar concerns.

How to define the proper limitations of political influence is a problem both for political theory and for the ethics of advertising as a dimension of business ethics. Should an advertising firm refuse to do ads for a candidate if it disapproves of the candidate's views? Does it matter if the disapproval is moral rather than, say, economic? And suppose one provides negative political ads. What restraints should be observed (beyond avoiding outright lies) in framing ads about an opposing candidate?

Reflective people differ about how to balance, on the one hand, the tendency of economic liberty to produce political and other inequalities and, on the other hand, the freedom and property rights that a flourishing democracy protects.[3] This balancing problem has at least two major aspects. One is largely constitutional and legal: it concerns what *laws* a free democracy should have to determine taxation and to protect economic freedom. Taxes are needed for defense, public works, and education (which is essential to guarantee equality of opportunity), but excessive taxation or regulation hampers business. This balancing problem is also *partly* ethical, since the notions of *just* laws—and of the human rights they must protect—are broadly ethical. The other aspect of the problem is fully ethical: what standards should *ethical* businesses *voluntarily* uphold? Both concerns are important for business ethics, but the latter is primary in this book. The next chapter will consider how businesses might ethically view their role in society *within* a framework of law such as exists in the United States and other countries: a framework intended to preserve both the equal citizenship rights of democracy and extensive economic freedom.

2

THE RIGHTS AND SOCIAL RESPONSIBILITIES OF BUSINESS

We have seen how property rights are basic supports of capitalism. How far do they go for owners of a business? One might think that we have absolute rights over things we own—not just the power to use or sell them, but also the power to destroy them. Not so. I may have these powers regarding an old car. But my rights to my land do not extend to poisoning it with chemical wastes. Nor may I use my car to run down other people. Others' rights limit ours.

The Moral Rights of Businesses

The rights of business owners, then, are not absolute. But one might think the only limitations on these rights are the negative kind imposed by others' rights, and that as long as others are not harmed in certain ways by our exercise of our rights, that exercise is ethical. We have to say "not harmed *in certain ways*" to make room for harming others—legitimately if unfortunately—by putting them out of business through offering better products at lower prices. Even our rights not to be harmed are not absolute, and it is intrinsic to free market societies to allow businesses to risk doing certain kinds of harm. Suffering economic harm by losing out to competitors is common in any well-functioning capitalist system. Are there, however, limitations on property rights which do *not* include avoiding harm to others?

At this point we again encounter the kind of difference regarding rights that stems partly from the different democratic traditions. On the one side is the free market neoclassical economics famously represented by the economist Milton Friedman and many others. He says that "in a free economy"

> [t]here is one and only one social responsibility of business...to increase its profits so long as it stays within the rules of the game, which is to say, engages in open and free competition without deception or fraud....Few trends could so thoroughly undermine the very foundations of our free society as the acceptance by corporate officials of a social responsibility other than to make as much money for their stockholders as possible.[4]

The underlying idea is that business managers—from chief executives down—are *agents* of the owners. They are employed to maximize return on investment, and their legitimate authority derives from the owners' will. This agency conception of management does not apply to managers who own the business they run; but our main concern is companies owned by non-managing stockholders. For owners who are managers, economic freedom entitles them to set their own goals.

In both cases—those of owners as management and those of stockholders to whom management is responsible—the free market perspective can support a *limited* role for government. Not to pay taxes, for instance, would hurt others by withholding a fair share of the funds government needs in order to protect the population and enforce contracts. But on the free market view, taxes are to be no greater than such limited purposes require.

Other views of the responsibilities of management are more hospitable to the egalitarian democratic tradition. These views include various partly or even mainly socialistic economic perspectives, but let us concentrate on the more common positions like those of *welfare capitalists,* i.e., those who believe in a free economy but also endorse tax-supported public education, national transportation, safety regulation of food, medicine, and utilities, and emergency funding for the unemployed. Most advanced contemporary capitalistic societies are welfarist to some degree. Welfare capitalism keeps the unemployed from starving and imposes taxes sufficient to achieve that. An *extreme* free market view would not tax businesses and citizens even for this purpose.

Welfare capitalism may be based on any of several rationales. One is that democracy should benefit *all* of the people and so should tax businesses and citizens in a way that funds an educational system that enables everyone to develop economically useful and personally rewarding skills. Another rationale is that even from an economic point of view, society as a whole is better off when government provides not only educational services, but a kind of "utility floor": healthcare, unemployment insurance, and other benefits. The former rationale stresses providing opportunities and some benefits for all, but not universal healthcare; the latter includes universal healthcare and more unemployment protection; and some welfarist positions provide more than the former and less than the latter.

A Proposal for Justifying Inequalities in Free Democracies

There are, then, many welfarist positions, from those that go only slightly beyond the free market view in welfare programs to those that are socialistic. Let us consider a view (developed by John Rawls) that provides a contrast with the pure free market view but also makes room for *both* capitalism and, apparently, a far-reaching welfare system. The view proposes two principles of justice appropriate for free democracies and bearing directly on the relation between business and society. They might be roughly formulated as follows:

1. *Equal basic liberty principle*: All are entitled to as much liberty as all can exercise without undermining the liberty of others.
2. *Difference principle*: Inequalities (e.g. in income or healthcare) are permissible only if (a) they attach to positions open to all by fair competition and (b) they are to the advantage of all, especially the least well off.[5]

A partial rationale for these principles (with principle 1 having almost absolute priority over principle 2 if they conflict) is as follows. First, because justice *requires* equal basic liberties (equality in the potential exercise of autonomy, roughly, in self-government), justice supports principle 1. Second, it supports principle 2 (even

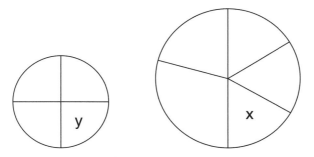

Figure 1

Uniform vs. larger shares of the welfare "pie."

if that is taken as *sufficient* to justify inequalities) because justice *allows* socioeconomic inequalities where everyone benefits: only from envy would one take less in order to avoid others' having more. Third, even (enlightened) *self-interest* supports the two principles: better to have the smallest slice of a bigger pie than one slice of an equally divided pie with smaller slices, provided one can—as the difference principle guarantees—freely compete for the large slices. Thus, in Figure 1, would you prefer y, an equal share of the smaller pie, or x, the smallest share of the bigger pie? Is equality in wealth worth enough to you to offset greater socioeconomic benefit you would lose? Might you—apart from being influenced by envy—even tolerate huge differences between your wealth and someone else's if the system allowing this still benefits you over one that reduces the possible distance between the largest and the smallest shares? The aim of social justice, on this view, is to protect everyone's liberty and to distribute profits made by the best off by a formula that benefits the worst off. This may mean high taxes (to benefit the worst off)—perhaps higher taxes than any actual capitalist society requires—but no one has shown that the plan prevents vast wealth.

The idea is that a just society—which a free democracy seeks to be—allows all the freedom citizens can have without impairing the liberty of others—all they can have *equally*. Inequalities in wealth are permitted, but, as one would expect in the egalitarian democratic tradition, they must be justifiable. Businesses can justify rejecting socialism and having a system that allows great wealth *provided* this benefits everyone, including the poor. But how could it? One answer is that the *incentives* provided by the chance to become wealthy and to build great institutional businesses results in productivity and invention that benefit society as a whole. Even the worst off might accept this, though they might also plausibly argue for *greater* protection than it gives them, say for a guarantee that they reach a certain *level* of welfare before anyone is allowed great wealth.

Determining Ethical Obligations: Some Major Approaches

We have so far considered the kind of society, and the sorts of laws, that are reasonable and just for a free capitalistic democracy. We should also examine the ethical as opposed to legal standards that are reasonable for ethical businesses in such a society. We naturally find that people sympathetic mainly with one or the other of the two democratic traditions tend to disagree. The more the ideal of equality influences us (as it will influence, e.g., many religious people who take to heart the idea that all people are children of God), the more we tend to think should be done for others who are substantially less fortunate than we. This is also the direction suggested by the idea that one should love one's neighbor as oneself (Matthew 22:37–39). There are, however, other ethical perspectives that bear on the ethical obligations of business. Let us consider several major ones.

Utilitarianism

For John Stuart Mill (the greatest nineteenth-century English philosopher), the master utilitarian principle is roughly this: choose that act from among your options which is best from the twin points of view of increasing human happiness and reducing human suffering:

> The creed which accepts as the foundation of morals "utility"...holds that actions are right in proportion as they tend to promote happiness, wrong as they tend to produce the

reverse of happiness. By happiness is intended pleasure, and the absence of pain.[6]

This formula does not tell us when an act is right, period; but the idea is that right acts contribute at least as favorably to the "proportion" of happiness to unhappiness (in the relevant population) as any alternative the agent has. Thus, if one act produces more happiness than another, it is preferable, other things equal. If the first also produces suffering, other things are not equal. We have to weigh good consequences of our projected acts against any bad consequences and, in appraising a prospective act, subtract its negative value from its positive value.[7]

Utilitarianism calls for maximization. To see why producing even a *lot* of good may not be not ethically sufficient, consider two points: (1) the more we have of what is good—good in itself, *basically* good—the better; (2) it is a mistake to produce less good than we can or, correspondingly, to reduce what is bad less than we can. Arguably, no good person would act suboptimally if this could be avoided.[8] Ideally, then, we would simultaneously produce pleasure *and* reduce pain. Often we cannot do both. A situation may be so dire that reducing pain is all we can do. For utilitarianism, although some people are better candidates to be made happy—or less unhappy—everyone matters morally.

On the plausible assumption that total happiness is best served by maintaining minimal well-being for the worst off, utilitarianism supports welfare capitalism. But it does not automatically support any highly specific position on the obligations of business. One might think otherwise if one identifies utilitarianism with the idea that ethics requires our producing the "greatest good for the greatest number." One reason utilitarianism does *not* imply any such thing is that great benefits (hence much good) to some, say college students, could quantitatively outweigh even the greatest benefits a business or government could provide for a larger number of people, say by tax cuts for the whole population.[9] Figure 2 makes this clear: the former, educational policy, could raise the *overall* happiness level (or lower the unhappiness level, or both) more than the latter, tax relief legislation, regardless of the smaller number of beneficiaries of the educational policy.

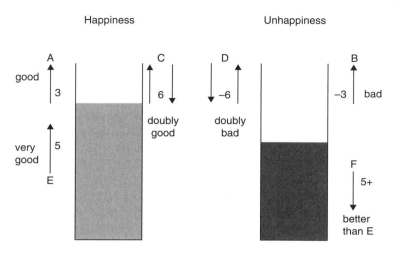

Figure 2

Utilitarianism: six types of act scored in terms of maximizing the "ratio" of the good (represented by the lighter shading) to the bad (represented by the darker shading).The containers represent the "quantities" of the good (happiness) and the bad (unhappiness) in the population (possibly all persons) whose well-being concerns the utilitarian. The letters represent acts considered; the length of the accompanying arrows—and the positive or negative numbers beside the acts— represent the positive or negative change in quantity of well-being the acts produce in the indicated direction. Act A is good; B is bad (hence its negative score). For acts C and D, let the left arrow represents the change produced in the happiness level and the right arrow represents the change produced in the unhappiness level. C, then, is doubly good, since it both increases happiness and decreases unhappiness; D is doubly bad, since it does the opposite. E is better than A, since it produces more happiness. Our obligation is to maximize the difference between the levels, favoring happiness (the lighter shading) over unhappiness (the darker shading). For a qualified utilitarian view that weights reducing unhappiness *higher* than increasing happiness, F might be better than E even if they produce the same *net* change in the ratio of the good to the bad.

How utilitarianism apparently supports welfare capitalism over other economic systems needs explanation. Here is a possible account. Arguably, businesses will contribute most favorably to human happiness (roughly, to the proportion of happiness to unhappiness in the world) by simply making a profit in a fair system of competition and paying taxes at a level high enough to support effective welfare programs and low enough to preserve incentives to gain wealth. For—given the incentives this arrangement might provide for talented people—it might not only support welfare programs but also lead to miracle drugs, fuel-efficient cars, superior fertilizers, and the like. Utilitarians may also argue that—at least if business leaders are utilitarians—then for both economic and ethical reasons, businesses operating in a welfare capitalist system will also contribute to the overall well-being of society through voluntary contributions, such as support for community projects, education, and the arts.

Rights-Based Ethics

A very different ethical approach takes off from the idea that the main ethical demand is that we act within our rights and accord other people theirs. On this view, right action is simply action within one's rights, whereas wrong action violates rights. Rights may be negative, for instance rights *not* to be harmed or deprived of free expression, or positive, say rights to be given what is promised you, including such things as emergency medical treatment if the government has guaranteed it. *Roughly speaking,* negative rights coincide with liberties, positive rights with entitlements to benefits.

From this perspective we can see how someone might ask: Why should businesses *have* to contribute to the well-being of society by doing anything positive for society? What right does government have to force taxation for this purpose, as opposed to police and military protection? Granted, our property rights are limited by obligations to support some government programs, most notably policing and defense, but once businesses pay their fair share of taxes for these, why should they do more?[10]

To this view, utilitarians and other *good-based* theorists may reply that even if businesses have a *right* not to do more, in the sense that their freedom not to do more should not be abridged by *compulsion*, they *ought* to do more. The plausible ethical point here is that a rights-based morality is unduly narrow. It takes what we ought (morally) to do to be only what we have no right not to do—presumably because someone else has a right to demand our doing it, in the sense that our not doing it violates that person's

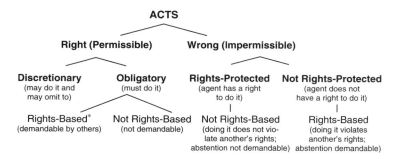

Figure 3

This figure shows an ethical classification of acts indicating how a rights-based ethics views obligation: our obligations lie *only* within others' rights against us. Most other ethical views recognize *wrongs within rights*, i.e., violations of obligations to others by acts that are *not* within their rights against us. Note that many right acts are discretionary (e.g., having coffee as opposed to tea) rather than obligatory (e.g., keeping a promise). Rights-based obligations—the *only* obligations under a rights-based ethics—lie in the starred category. Wrongs within rights are shown in the *rights-protected* category; e.g., giving nothing to charity may be wrong, though within one's rights and not *demandable* by charities. Unlike promise-keeping, it is a non–rights-based obligation and may be wrong, though within one's rights and not *demandable* by charities.

rights. All else is discretionary, as shown in Figure 3. In reality, however, we can and do distinguish between what we ought and ought not to do even *within* the sphere of our rights. Take a simple example: relations with coworkers. Our coworkers have a right to some consideration, say to being given at least minimal cooperation, but we *ought* to do more to support them than the minimum they can claim as their right.

It is not just utilitarians who think that ethics calls on us to do things we have a right not to do. This will be apparent from an outline of two other plausible and widely held ethical views: Kantianism and virtue ethics.

Kantian Ethics

The great eighteenth-century German philosopher Immanuel Kant held that we should always act in such a way that we can rationally will the principle we are acting on to be a universal law:

> So act as if the maxim of your action [that is, the principle of
> conduct underlying the action] were to become through your
> will a universal law of nature.[11]

This "Categorical Imperative" implies that I should not leave someone to bleed to death on the roadside if I could not rationally will the universality of the practice—say, even where *I* am the victim. We would not want to universalize, and thus live by, the callous principle: one should stop for someone bleeding to death provided it requires no self-sacrifice. Similarly, I should not make a lying promise to repay borrowed money if I could not rationally universalize my underlying principle, say that when I can get money only by making a lying promise, I will do this. One way to see why the Imperative apparently disallows this is to note that we *count on* promises from others and cannot rationally endorse the universality of a deceitful promissory practice that would victimize us.

Kant also gave a less abstract formulation of the Categorical Imperative:

> Act so that you use humanity, as much in your own person as in
> the person of every other, always at the same time as an end and
> never merely as a means.[12]

The idea is roughly that we must treat people as valuable in themselves, never merely as means to some end of ours. We are never to *use* people—including low-level, readily replaceable employees—as in manipulatively lying to them. Treating people as ends clearly requires caring about their good. They matter as persons, and we must at times and to some extent act *for their sake,* whether or not we benefit from it.[13]

Virtue Ethics

Virtue ethics differs from both utilitarianism and Kantianism in not being *rule centered.* Instead of proposing rules of conduct, it demands that we concentrate on being good as persons. Be honest, just, kind, and honorable, for instance. Thus, the ancient Greek philosopher Aristotle described just acts as the kind that a just person would perform. He did not define a just person as one who performs just acts, nor as one who follows certain rules.[14] He apparently considered moral traits of character ethically more basic than moral acts and moral rules. He said, regarding the types of acts that are right: "Actions are called just or temperate when they are the sort that a just or temperate person would do."[15] Similar virtue-ethical ideas are also found in non-Western traditions, such as Confucian ethics, especially as represented by the ancient Chinese philosopher Mencius.

For a virtue ethics, then, agents and their traits, as opposed to rules of action, are morally basic. Virtue ethics would have us ask both what kind of person we want to be and how we want to be seen by those we care about, say friends and family. Who wants to be (correctly) seen as cheap, insensitive, or even just indifferent to others' suffering? Who does not want to be seen as generous, caring, and fair?

One could say that virtue ethics endorses *be-rules* (be just, be honest, be kind) in contrast with *do-rules* (keep your promises). But, suggestive as it is, this contrast is misleading since be-rules do not make clear reference to *how* to fulfill their demands. We cannot fulfill be-rules without some prior knowledge of what to *do*. (It is because this point is understood that virtue ethics is often seen to require a good upbringing with definite kinds of acts prescribed for children.) The positive idea underlying virtue ethics is that we are to understand what it is to behave justly through studying the nature and tendencies of the just person, not the other way around. We do not, for instance, define just deeds as those that, say, treat people equally, and then define a just person as one who characteristically does such deeds.

Thus, for adults as well as for children, and in ordinary life as in business, *role models* are absolutely crucial for moral learning. Virtue ethics is indeed a kind of ethics of role modeling: good role models are *sources*, as well as potential teachers, of ethical standards. Rules of action can be formulated by generalizing from observations of virtuous agents, such as team leaders in a sales division; but the basic ethical standard is character rather than rules of action.

One value of the virtue approach to business ethics is that leadership in business is partly a role-modeling function. To call for conduct of any kind—but especially ethical conduct—when we do not exhibit it ourselves is at best unlikely to succeed and often hypocritical too. Good role modeling, as any major ethical view can stress, is both instructive and motivating.

Common-Sense Ethical Pluralism

Many readers will find something plausible in each of the approaches just sketched. Might a less abstract, more definite view capture much of the best in each? Utilitarianism above all requires good deeds; rights-based views stress respecting freedom, keeping commitments, and protecting property; Kantianism demands respecting others and acting on principles that accord with this respect; and virtue ethics demands such ethical decisions as are made by people who are, say, just, honest, and beneficent. There are many standards here, but they are not too numerous to be reflected in ordinary principles that morally decent people teach their children and generally follow.

These ordinary ethical principles (1) prohibit injustice, harming others, lying, and breaking promises and (2) positively, call for doing good deeds toward others and for efforts toward self-improvement. They do not require *maximizing* good consequences, but do require at least certain good deeds we can do without great self-sacrifice. Thus, fraudulent accounting, as lying, is prohibited; providing for employees' healthcare, up to some reasonable point, is, as doing good deeds, an obligation of most companies.

Most people find these principles intuitively plausible, and the view that such principles are directly knowable on the basis of reflection on their content—intuitively knowable—is called *ethical intuitionism.* It is considered a common-sense view because these and a few other principles seem to be a common-sensical core toward which the best ethical theories converge.[16] Since common-sense intuitionism is presented in Chapter 4, no further comment is needed here. It must simply be included among the perspectives from which to view the task of determining the ethical responsibilities of business.

Many who reflect on ethics find something of value in all the approaches just described, especially virtue ethics, Kantianism, and utilitarianism. Might a single wide principle include much of their content and encompass much of the common-sense plurality of obligations just indicated? There are apparently at least three conceptually independent factors that a sound ethical view should take into account: happiness, which we may think of as welfare conceived in terms of pleasure, pain, and suffering; justice, conceived largely as requiring equal treatment of persons; and freedom. On this approach—call it *pluralist universalism*—our broadest moral principle would require standards of conduct that optimize happiness as far as possible without producing injustice or curtailing freedom (including one's own). This principle is to be *internalized*—roughly, automatically presupposed and normally also strongly motivating—in a way that yields moral virtue. Right acts would be roughly those that conform to standards—including the ones described in Chapter 4—whose internalization and mutual balancing achieve that end. Each value (happiness, justice, and freedom) becomes, then, a guiding standard, and mature moral agents will develop a sense of how to act (or at least how to reach a decision to act) when the values pull in different directions.[17]

Pluralist universalism is triple-barreled. It implies that no specific, single standard can be our sole moral guide. This is especially so in the case of principles (like this one) that appeal to different and potentially conflicting elements. How should we balance these in the triple-barreled principle? A priority rule for achieving a balance among the three values—and among the common-sense principles that pluralist universalism helps to unify—is this. Considerations of justice and freedom take priority (at least normally) over considerations of happiness; justice and freedom do not conflict because justice requires the highest level of freedom possible within the limits of peaceful coexistence, and this is as much freedom as any reasonable ideal of liberty demands. Thus, public sale of a drug that gives people pleasure but reduces their freedom would be prohibited by the triple-barreled principle (apart from, say, special medical uses); a social policy (say, draft exemptions for all who have a high-school education) that makes most citizens happy but causes great suffering for a minority (who must go to war) would be rejected as unjust. Moreover, although one may voluntarily devote one's life to enhancing human happiness (if only by reducing human suffering), this is not obligatory. Thus, coercive force may not be used to produce even such highly desirable beneficence.

Ethical Obligations and Legal Requirements

Ethics requires more of us than does any reasonable body of laws. It also calls on us to more than simply observe others' rights. But why should we, in business or elsewhere, do more than is demanded by the law or the rights of others? Kant's view (among others) indicates why. Suppose I own a highly profitable real estate firm. If I make no charitable contributions in my community, I do not violate anyone's rights and I live within mine. Kant might say that although I am not using anyone *merely as a means*—as I would if I employed untrained, unsuspecting people to remove asbestos from a building I am selling—I am *also* not treating fellow citizens *as ends*. I do nothing for their good (beyond what my taxes may do for them). I may defend my conduct by saying that their rights in the matter end with *requesting*, as opposed to demanding, my contributions. It is true that I have freedom rights to retain my profits and give nothing to any charity. But is doing so ethical? If I have no excuse, such as a sick child who needs expensive treatments, am I not criticizable as ethically deficient?

On any plausible virtue ethics, morality also calls for doing more than one must in order to avoid violating anyone's rights. Generosity is a virtue. So is *beneficence,* understood as the disposition to do good deeds toward others. Compassionate caring, which is stressed in many religious traditions and prominently in some, say in Catholic social teaching and in some of Hindu ethics, may also count as a virtue. These virtues would be unfulfilled by my retaining all my profits. To be sure, for Kantian and virtue ethics, as for pluralist universalism, we need not make contributions in such a way as to *maximize* human happiness, as utilitarianism requires. These views are not quantitative in that way and are also less demanding of beneficent conduct than is utilitarianism. But they do call for doing more for others than we would do if we did only what, like paying our debts, we have no right *not* to do.[18]

Treating others as ends, like being beneficent toward others—which is an element in so treating them—is a matter of judgment. Ethics allows us to balance such demands against those of our private ambitions. Aristotle held that we should seek a "Golden Mean" between excess and deficiency: giving away every penny is prodigal, likely leaving one unable to contribute a still greater amount later; giving nothing is selfish. The mean is not numerical. Its discovery may require reflection. One role of *conscience* is to keep us focused on whether we have optimally steered between excess and deficiency.

It should now be clear that ethics calls on us not only to do things the *law* does not require, but also to do things that no one else's *rights* require. Where no one has a right to our help, we may still properly believe we should give it. Indeed, what principle would we want others to abide by if we suddenly had an accident but no one *owed* us assistance? As Kant would stress, a reasonable principle is that, within the limits of our powers and major commitments, we should render aid. Even if a business is enormous and is only a legal person, through its management it has agency and is subject to ethical standards. Even without idealization or the high standards a religion may bring to the operation of a business, ethics calls on businesses to do more than is strictly required by either law or the rights of the persons and communities with which it deals.

3

THE CONSTITUENCIES
OF ETHICAL BUSINESS

In a capitalistic democracy, businesses inevitably have both legal obligations to government and ethical responsibilities to society. Defenders of capitalistic democracy differ about how *much* business owes government—say in taxes—and also about the extent of its moral responsibility to society. Is that responsibility, for instance, negative and mainly a matter of avoiding harm to others, or is the responsibility also positive, extending to supporting charities, providing services such as computer maintenance in schools, restoring forests after devastating fires, and the like?

Limitations of Ownership Rights

Businesses are *owned,* whether they are small and privately held or large and publicly traded. This is one reason why, though businesses are *agents* in society, they are only "legal persons." Persons are not owned.[19] It is they who are owners, and they have far-reaching rights over what they own. These property rights are not, however, absolute. How far do they go in determining the ethical responsibilities of management?

For a strong version of the free market view of business in society, the central positive obligation of managers as such, i.e., *in* their managerial capacity, is to serve the interests of the owners. On the free market view, doing this requires maximizing return on investment—roughly, profit. But notice three points.

First, profit cannot be taken to be the *sole* interest stockholders have in a company they own. Often they have some desire for "socially responsible investing," which requires investing only in companies that do not commit certain kinds of unethical acts, such as polluting the environment.[20]

Second, stockholders commonly do not express their interests to management (though this pattern is beginning to change). The result is that management must determine these as best it can. How far should management go to ascertain the priorities of stockholders? Is one yearly mailing to stockholders enough to provide a chance to express these priorities? Might there be more frequent electronic consultation? Should there be a standing committee—other than the Board of Directors—to represent rank-and-file stockholders and exercise certain powers in the company? There are many possibilities.[21]

The Interests of Stockholders

A third consideration concerns what constitutes the "interests" of stockholders. The notion of serving interests (whether of stockholders or others) allows managers much latitude. There may be a number of ways to maximize profit which, though economically equivalent, have very different effects on society, including other countries. The Merck Pharmaceutical Company, for instance, expended millions of dollars to combat river blindness. Merck developed Mectizan, which, in a single tablet annually, could relieve symptoms and prevent advance of the disease. The ultimate financial results were apparently positive, though the company could not initially count on avoiding financial loss. There are other ways to do something that pleases long-term investors even if it requires *some* short-term decrease in profits. An example is Johnson & Johnson's recalling all its Tylenol tablets when some had been tampered with, causing several deaths. *At least* short-term profits were reduced, but most investors were gratified by the commitment to public safety that led to the recall and made tamper-proof packaging a norm. The recall decision is sometimes cited as a paradigm of *corporate integrity*.

So far, we have assumed that the positive ethical obligations of managers are owed mainly to owners (stockholders in the most common cases). We have also seen that this need not limit their choices to just those that maximize profits. But recall that ownership rights are neither absolute nor—more important here—the sole basis of moral standards concerning property. There are (as shown in Chapter 2) things we ought to do that, strictly speaking, we have a right not to do.

One manifestation of the point that our ethical responsibilities are not definable in terms of rights can be seen even within the strong free market view. Part of this position is the *shareholder view of managerial responsibility* (stockholders are shareholders, but "shareholder" is used here because it applies to joint ownerships, as with certain partnerships or family businesses, that do not involve stock). This is the view that managers are agents of owners and must above all maximize profits. But first, shareholders themselves may want or even ask for more than just profit maximization, even if that is what they want most. Second, even if they ask only for maximum profit, management still has latitude concerning *how* profits are maximized. Some ways are ethically better than others, or more in line with the overall interests or shareholders, or both. It turns out, then, that even the shareholder view does not require management to have a narrow conception of its ethical responsibilities. The shareholder view, however, is open to plausible challenges we must consider.

The Multiple-Constituency View of the Corporation

There is little doubt that human beings have moral rights not to be harmed and that these are strong enough to limit shareholders' rights to have management maximize profits. But why must managerial ethics focus mainly on shareholder rights in the first place? *One* way to look at this is in relation to the positive rights of groups of people other than owners, where "positive rights" are rights to be treated well or given certain benefits, as opposed to the negative rights we have considered—above all, the right not to be harmed.

Granting that owners are essential for managerial responsibility, consider the second main group of constituents—employees (including managers). They have a right to be treated with respect: not just with civility but as persons with interests, feelings, and vulnerabilities. Third, there are customers and clients. They have a right to be treated not only with respect—which implies avoiding deceptiveness—but also with some concern to satisfy their interests and not merely to make a profit on them. Fourth, there are suppliers of goods or services. A business may have an ongoing relationship with suppliers in which there is the kind of trust that leads suppliers to extend credit to the business, to management's being loyal to suppliers, and sometimes to one side or both giving the other special privileges.

Ongoing relationships are a major basis of mutual rights. The closer and more longstanding the relationship, the stronger the positive rights tend to be. In close relationships, even if only in doing business, we tend to make promises or communicate assurances to one another; we certainly give rise to legitimate expectations. These are important kinds of *rights-conferring actions*. The rights in question include suppliers' rights to consideration, say in a client company's decision to relocate to a place the supplier cannot reach.

A fifth category of people to whom business is responsible is creditors. They have put something at risk for the company and thereby also have a special right to consideration and, sometimes, to information not given to the public at large.

The sixth case ethical management must consider is the "community," the network of groups surrounding a business. Take first local employees and others affected by noise, traffic, or pollution. From the mid-twentieth century through the mid-1990s, Nepera, Inc., which produced chemicals in Woodbury, New York, gave off malodorous smoke that sometimes caused closure of a local school—a violation of community rights. The plant closed in 2006, but this did not solve the problem. The surrounding ground still required extensive pumping to remove wastes.

We should also consider community services, from roads to utilities, schools, libraries, and recreation. Are there not some relationships here that ground positive rights of one or another community group? Teachers and city workers, for instance, regularly serve a company indirectly. Normally, these groups include some people who do more than the strict minimum legally required. Granted, the negative rights of communities are more prominent than their positive rights. Moreover, some companies may have little contact with the community. They may be small or, even if large, have their work done, as an insurance company may, chiefly by agents using small offices spread across a large region.

Despite these qualifications, communities or, similarly, segments of the public on which a company depends will be one among the other five constituencies mentioned. There may be still other constituencies, including an entire national population in the case of a company like Microsoft, whose products or services affect nearly everyone. The ethical point here is that there are many groups with not only negative rights affecting a company but positive rights of a kind that, at a minimum, ground a *legitimate interest*—a morally proper interest as opposed to a mere psychological concern—in the company. This interest implies that management has an ethical responsibility both to treat the groups with respect and to give them some consideration in many company decisions, above all those that affect the group in question.

Constituents as "Stakeholders"

The six constituency groups just identified are usually considered the main (often overlapping) "stakeholders" in a company. A "stakeholder theory" of corporate responsibility may have much the same thrust as the multiple constituency view: to imply that business has ethical responsibilities to others besides owners.[22] A constituent of a business, however, is someone with positive as well as negative rights in relation to management—and owners. Positive rights include at least the minimal rights to be considered in company decisions. These rights go with having a legitimate interest, but businesses normally confer further rights on such groups as suppliers and consumers. They promise payments to the former and products or services to the latter. Moreover, these rights of non-owners limit the rights of ownership. How *much* they do so differs from one company to another (and will be explored later).

It is important to reiterate, however, that although rights are immensely important in ethics, they do not generally *determine*, though they do limit, just what we ought to do. Some moral responsibilities toward others—and especially toward one's constituents—are not grounded in their rights. Even if my supplier of raw material does not have a right to know in advance that I am moving to a cheaper source, and even if I will only slightly reduce the supplier's income, I *ought* to provide the earliest notice I reasonably can. Moreover, the obligation tends to be stronger in proportion to how long and how personal the relationship is.

Given that the terminology of stakeholders has gained wide currency, something should be said about why we might often prefer speaking of constituencies and responsibilities to those groups. In part, this is because proponents of a stakeholder view of the corporation have often (and influentially) put their main point in terms of at least two contrasting notions: (1) those who are "affected" by or can affect a business and (2) those conceived as in some way ethically warranting concern. Neither idea is adequately clear, and the stakeholder view is plausible largely through the force of the main examples of stakeholders commonly cited—those listed above—and through the root metaphor of a stakeholder as someone who has driven a stake into the ground to mark off a plot of properly claimed land.[23]

The category of those who are affected by a company or can affect it is too wide to help us without major qualifications. It makes regulatory agencies prime stakeholders since they have power over businesses. It includes people who may be affected by charitable contributions a company could make abroad where it does not even have employees or appreciable sales. It even includes would-be thieves, since they can dramatically affect it. It also includes competitors who suffer from reduced profits as a result of losing out in fair competition.

We should also notice at least three important underlying ideas that affect thinking about stakeholders. First, there is the common idea of having a *stake in* something. This is roughly having an interest in it, usually with something to lose, as one might have a stake in expanding a community library one uses. The idea is closely related to a second notion, having something *at stake.* This does not entail investing or even doing anything. Residents near a chemical company have much at stake in relation to its pollution control. Third, there is the root notion of *staking a claim,* as in the cases of property acquisition Locke must have imagined, where one drives stakes around land one is farming to lay claim to the harvest.

All three notions *suggest* how a legitimate interest may arise from the activity of *staking a claim* or from putting something *at stake* or from *having a stake* in the success of a venture or company, but none of these notions guarantees having a *legitimate* interest. People can stake illegitimate claims; they can have a stake in an illegal and immoral gambling house; and they can have much at stake in a neighbor's selling a house to somebody they bigotedly dislike.

These points do not imply that we should never talk of stake-holders. The metaphor of driving proprietary stakes around a piece of land has suggestive value. But a suggestive metaphor may lead to exaggerating the understanding it provides. Business ethics must clarify the notion of a *legitimate* interest in a company and the related concept of a *justified* stake in it. We must ask, then, what ethical responsibilities managers have, to whom, and of what strength. The idea of multiple constituencies helps to focus on this question, but there remains much to say to clarify it. For the present, we have established at least this: there is such a thing as "corporate social responsibility" (CSR), and it is not merely negative but includes responsibilities to take account of various constituencies. How to determine these responsibilities is a difficult task, to which the remaining chapters are partly devoted.

4

A FRAMEWORK FOR MAKING
ETHICAL DECISIONS

We have seen that the ethical responsibilities of business are not exhausted by owner's rights or even by the negative rights of society or of the constituencies of business. There are various things business managers ought to do that are not rights-based at all and concern at least the six specified constituent ("stakeholder") groups: owners, employees (including management), customers and clients, suppliers, creditors, and the community (or communities) where a business operates. Given scarce resources and limited time, however, it is often unclear just what management ought to do regarding one or another constituency. It would be naïve to offer a formula for determining this, but we can frame wide-ranging standards to guide ethical decisions. These standards are broad enough and flexible enough to apply to any kind of ethical decision.

Common-Sense Ethical Principles

Many ethical theories provide principles of conduct. We have considered two of the most important: Kantian and utilitarian theories. Even more widely known is the Golden Rule, which appears in both Eastern and Western traditions.[24] The same holds for the Ten Commandments, whose non-religious ethical imperatives—such as the prohibitions of killing, lying, and theft—are equivalent to principles also supported by non-religious moral approaches. Virtue ethics does not directly provide principles of action; but for any plausible moral principle, there is some virtue whose proper exercise tends to lead to the same actions required by the principle. For the principle that we should not lie, there is the virtue of veracity; for the principle that we should not oppress, that of justice; and so forth. A good case can be made that there is a universally valid set of ethical principles that are reflected both in major ethical theories, such as the three just noted, and in at least many of the major religions of the world.[25]

To see what the common-sense moral principles are, we do well to begin with W. D. Ross's famous list of "prima facie" obligations:[26]

1. *Justice*: the double-barreled obligation (a) negatively, not to commit injustice and (b) positively, to prevent future injustices and rectify existing ones;
2. *Non-injury*: the obligation to avoid harming others;
3. *Fidelity*: the obligation to keep promises;
4. *Veracity*: the obligation to avoid lying (veracity and fidelity constitute kinds of fidelity understood as keeping faith—both 3. and 4. are *faithfulness to our word*);
5. *Reparation*: the obligation to make amends for wrong-doing;
6. *Beneficence*: the obligation to do good deeds for others, especially to contribute to their virtue (goodness of character), knowledge, or pleasure;
7. *Self-improvement*: the obligation to better oneself;
8. *Gratitude*: the obligation to express appreciation for good deeds toward us.

These obligations are prima facie in a special way: they have a moral force that, though overridable, is not completely eliminated even when (as will be illustrated) it is overridden by conflicting obligations of higher priority. Two of the obligations may need clarification. Consider injustice first. Injustice is not just any kind of wrong-doing, but above all either unfair distribution, as where people are paid differently only because of race or gender, or undeserved punishment. Second, take reparation. This is "repair" after such things as destruction of property or causing injury, as where one negligently installs a boiler that later explodes.

None of the eight obligations is absolute in an ordinary sense of that term: having *finality*, i.e., always being what, all things considered (hence "finally"), one ought to do. For instance, in an economic slump, fidelity and beneficence to longstanding employees might result in (financially) harming some recently hired workers who must be laid off to avoid bankruptcy. Our final obligation here is one of combined fidelity and beneficence, and *in this case* it outweighs the obligation of non-injury owed to those recently hired.

Final obligation, then, is determined *relative to circumstances.* This does not imply *relativism,* in the sense entailing that there are no objective, cross-culturally justified actions *even when circumstances are taken into account.* Indeed, in two limited ways all the obligations may be plausibly considered absolute (universally valid)—in *standing* and in *valence.* First, even though they are prima facie and can be overridden, they always matter: they always have *moral standing.* Even breaking a minor promise has some *weight*—which is why one must normally explain or apologize for it. Second, they are *valenced,* implying a positive or negative reason for action, even if a minor reason. For instance, that an act would be a lie always counts against it; that another act would be a good deed (beneficent) always counts for it.[27]

I propose two other kinds of obligation as having a similar ethical status:

9. *Liberty*: the obligation to preserve and enhance human freedom;

10. *Respectfulness*: the category of obligations of *manner* (roughly, of respectfulness).

The obligations of respectfulness are special: they concern *how* we do what we are obligated to do under other principles, as opposed to *what* we must do in some way or other—obligations of *matter.*

These principles are confirmed by unbiased moral reflection on how we ourselves want to be treated. That is not to deny, however, that they may be rationalized by, or even in some way derived from, a more comprehensive moral principle or set of principles, perhaps including the pluralist universalism formulated in Chapter 2. This principle treats justice, liberty, and happiness as the three most basic values that such specific ethical principles as the ten in question must uphold.[28] What we must now do, however, is less theoretical. It is to see how these ten common-sense principles figure in a strategy of decision for business ethics.

A Five-Step Model for Making Difficult Ethical Decisions

If the ten principles just formulated constitute an adequately comprehensive summary of our moral obligations, and if they can be integrated with various ethical theories, they provide a good starting point for making difficult ethical decisions. What follows will be a model (in a non-formal sense of the term) for proceeding on the basis of the commonly presupposed, intuitive ethical framework just sketched.

1. *Classification*

The guiding question here is: What are my obligations in this case? The appropriate response to this question is to determine what obligations apply, hence to identify initial, first-stage options. Is the case, for example, one of conflicting obligations, say a conflict between loyalty to one person and justice to another? A moral problem normally arises because we become aware of certain facts, say that we must either risk losing a business or lay off some good employees. Such facts present moral problems precisely because they ground conflicting obligations. It is facts of this kind—obligation-implying facts—that we particularly need for ethical decisions.

One reason we need such facts is that morality, as a framework for harmonious, coordinated human life, is plainly focused on regulating the impact of our actions on human beings and, to a lesser extent, on other living beings and even our environment. Another reason is that facts of these kinds enable us to view our options in relation to major ethically relevant categories. In the light of such facts, we can classify a problem as concerning, say, issues of competing claims under the heading of justice (a conflict within a single category of obligation); of fidelity as opposed to beneficence (a cross-category conflict); of self-improvement as opposed to gratitude (gratitude may call for some self-sacrifice); and so on for the ten obligations described above. Beneficence might call for seeking a comprehensive healthcare plan. Fidelity to shareholders might call for saving money by choosing a narrower one.

We may or may not have all the needed facts when confronted with a problem. To increase the chance that we do, we may ask, regarding each basic obligation and any context in which we face a moral problem, whether that obligation is present. One question, then, is whether justice is at stake. Another is whether someone would be harmed by a decision we might make. Still another is whether we have commitments (most obviously through promises or contracts) that affect the matter. Some kinds of obligations will be obviously irrelevant; for some fortunate people, obligations of reparation arise only infrequently: harming or wronging others may be quite rare for them. There is no limit, however, to the variety of ways in which the basic obligations can generate challenging conflicts.

We usually do not have to go through all ten questions corresponding to the ten basic obligations in order to see which obligations are relevant. It is often quite clear what the problem is, say a conflict between loyalty to an employer who counts on one to uphold company values and loyalty to a fellow employee who has violated a company rule and told one in confidence. An experienced person may in fact see the relevant conflict(s) virtually immediately on considering the question of what to do. Commonly, considerations of beneficence and, on the other side, non-injury are relevant to moral decisions; and business decisions often result in benefits for some and setbacks for others, if only competitors. Business decisions by their very nature have the potential to produce significant good or bad effects. Once we bring the relevant questions to bear on a decision problem, we can determine what obligations apply. This will enable us to classify our problem in relation to the obligations bearing on it.

2. *Identification of Conflicts of Obligations*

A guiding question here is: What conflicting (prima facie) obligations are in tension? This step identifies the main ethical problem: if there were only one obligation, or if all our obligations pointed to the same thing, we would have no ethical problem about what to do—though we might have a problem about *how*. If our classification of relevant obligations in a decision situation is adequate, we should be able to articulate any conflicts between sets of obligations that apply. For any difficult moral decision, there will be conflicting considerations, if only in a single category of obligation, as where there is a choice between recognizing one rather than another excellent employee with a promotion (a matter of justice), or between two good charities that each serve the needy (a matter of beneficence).

Even where there is no conflict about what course of action fulfills one's final obligation, say promoting one person over another, there might remain problems about what specific acts will best accomplish this goal. Making a promotion may involve self-sacrifice, great effort, or ill effects, such as resentment on the part of a person not promoted. With promotions, there are questions of timing, salary increment, conditions of the new position, and others. Some of these questions are ethical and go beyond efficiency. Competing obligations may pull in different directions for any of these kinds of acts.

Conflicts of obligation may persist even when an action emerges as best. For there may still be an ethical problem regarding the right *manner* in which to carry it out. The search for the right way to do something intended is analogous to the search for a good means to do it at all, and it can be equally substantive. Persuading a proud small business owner to accept a loan may be one's means to fulfilling an obligation; how to do it without wounding pride may be a challenge. And if we promote only one of two good candidates for a position, what (if anything) should we say to the other? It is commonly presupposed that practical ethical problems, including "ethical dilemmas"—cases in which two or more incompatible options seem obligatory—concern what *act* to perform, such as whether to offer a loan or make a promotion. But life is full of cases where it is the *manner* of an action that is in question: some ways of doing the right thing are wrong, and sometimes the right thing should be delayed, reconsidered, or revised in the light of the limited ways in which we can realistically do it.

3. *Ethical Assessment of the Obligations*

Again, there is a guiding question: How *weighty* are the conflicting obligations? We should appraise the importance, in the context of decision, of each obligation involved, for instance determining the seriousness of a promise and the importance of the consequences of breaking it, by comparison with the consequences of helping others instead. Normally, we cannot strictly quantify the positives and negatives; but numbers can be used to represent the intuitive importance of one or another consideration.

A sense of typical *preponderance* (i.e., prevailing over competing obligations) as opposed to *automatic priority* over other obligations may also be useful. We may, for instance, regard attending to a very sick person as generally having priority over keeping a promise to finish a repair job on time. But even here we must be cautious and seek a *reflective equilibrium*: a state of mind in which our descriptive factual beliefs about a case are in balance with our moral judgments and our principles bearing on the case. This may be achieved where, guided by the ten principles described above, we determine a promotion on the basis of a comparative study of an employee's performance in the light of both company goals and peer achievement.

Given how commonly an ethical assessment requires comparison of conflicting prima facie obligations of the kinds we are exploring, it may be desirable to formulate a working principle that incorporates the comparison. It might be a rough principle to the effect that when one has to choose between retaining a loyal employee and risking loss of the business, avoiding the latter is the greater obligation. As we shall see, one might approach decisions with many other, more specific principles.

This is a good place to contrast the framework proposed here with what we might call *ethics by cost-benefit analysis,* such as a certain kind of utilitarianism would endorse. Consider the Ford Pinto case. The Pinto had its gas tank in the rear in a way that made dangerous fires more likely in rear-end collisions. Suppose that a business takes money as the only relevant "good." Then management calculates the probability of accidents in which the tanks result in losses through, say, lawsuits and bad publicity, and one multiplies this probability by the estimated average loss. Suppose the probability of such accidents given the usage expected for the Pinto yields 500 anticipated accidents with an average loss of $600,000. The expected loss, then, for Pinto rear-end collisions is $600,000 × 500: $300,000,000. This loss might be less than the cost of recall or (depending on how far along the production is) redesign. Suppose redesign would cost $400,000,000. The cost-effective decision, then, is not to redesign; and if no separate value is assigned to death or injury, this is what the company will do.

Utilitarians use the same kind of calculation strategy, but they put happiness in place of profit and pain in place of loss and then try to quantify happiness in terms of the best indications they can find, such as socioeconomic indications of material well-being and people's reports of their level of happiness.[29] By contrast with both decision strategies, the one proposed in this chapter takes *all* violations of obligations negatively and all fulfillments of them positively, and it uses balanced judgment (possibly assisted by numbers) to determine the final decision.

4. *Selection of Ethically Viable Options*

Once an assessment of the conflicting obligations is done, the guiding question is: What are the ethically viable alternatives? There may be only one. In view of the best comparative assessment we can make, we should seek the ethically best alternative(s) and formulate a *way* to do the deed(s) in question. Here obligations of manner come in, sometimes yielding a further ethical problem. It may seem clear that, for example, my (final) obligation is to give someone a negative performance evaluation. But suppose the person is psychologically weak. I may initially find no way to fulfill the obligation without violating a strong obligation of non-injury. If, however, I recognize an obligation to do the evaluation *supportively* (an obligation of manner), I may then be able to fulfill the basic obligation—to give a negative report—without unacceptable injury.

We have seen how ethical problems characteristically embody conflicting (prima facie) obligations and how comparisons may yield practical principles that provide major premises for practical decision. But particularly for experienced people, reflection on the facts may sometimes quickly indicate one option. It may be clear on reflection that one obligation is primary. Figure 4 provides a way to conceive such a problem. The weights represent

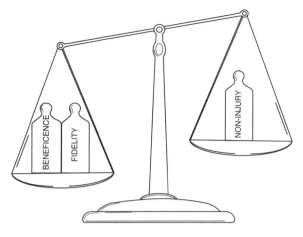

Figure 4

Here a conflict of prima facie obligations is represented (for the basic case of two competing options) by a balance scale. The drawing represents the obligations of beneficence and fidelity together outweighing an obligation of non-injury. The former two might favor releasing an employee who cannot easily find a comparable job; the latter would favor retention. Similar conflicts may occur in a single category of obligation, say beneficence to employees vs. beneficence toward stockholders. Notice that the obligation of non-injury, though *outweighed*, does not disappear. It may indeed generate a "residual" obligation, say to help the person to find another job.

the conflicting obligations; their size indicates their strength; and the lower plate shows the final ("weightiest") obligation. Here beneficence and fidelity to one's managerial role might outweigh the obligation not to hurt the employee, and their greater weight indicates the final obligation, say to terminate employment. The diagram also shows that although the prima facie obligation of non-injury is *outweighed*, it is not eliminated. Its presence explains why I have the secondary, follow-up obligation to handle the hurt beneficently, say by having a senior coworker explain that criticism is ultimately for the person's good.

A principle, new or old, may or may not be formulated in the light of reflection on an ethical problem. Just as a literary critic can judge a poem without formulating the criteria that guide the judgment, an ethical person of practical wisdom can frame a judgment that is grounded in moral reasons whether or not it is reached by an episode of practical reasoning with premises in which those reasons figure. This seems possible particularly for people who combine moral virtue and long experience. It is also possible for people applying a principle—say the principle that criticism should be given delicately—that they have internalized and can follow without bringing it to consciousness. More commonly, however, moral problems cannot be resolved without comparing options and engaging in practical reasoning in which one or another moral consideration figures.

5. *Decision on a Course of Action*

The first four stages call for reflection on the case; this one calls for a decision that resolves it. If only one option emerges in adequately considering the problem, a decision may be made immediately. But where competing options remain after initial reflection (as is common), the need is to formulate a resolutive judgment. I might, for instance, realize that a proxy could do the evaluation I am obligated to do, but without the bad consequences I myself would produce. This idea might arise as I seek a good means to the goal governing the decision making. The search for a means may alter the end. This instrumental search may help with a moral problem by leading us to modify the end, as where one decides that a proxy could fulfill the basic values underlying the obligation to do the evaluation.

A working principle for business decisions might be far more detailed. Consider one for hiring. Given competing candidates for a single promotion, your principle—meant to be usable in justifying the decision as well as in making it—could take account of (1) experience, (2) productivity, (3) support from managers and peers, and (4) replaceability in case of resignation (a market factor). You might have a rough weighting of these variables (so that numbers can be assigned for explicitness), but it is common simply to compare such variables intuitively. Suppose, however, that two candidates are equally qualified by (1) through (4). You might then use a principle mandating a coin flip or, as in some common cases, a principle on which minority status tips the balance until the organization reaches a certain diversity level. (This "affirmative action" preference for minorities will be discussed in Chapter 8.)

If the search for a means may alter the end, the entire process of reflecting on a difficult moral case may lead, not to the single resolution we first aimed at, but to a twofold course of action. We might, for example, decide *both* to promote one candidate, thereby solving the initial decision problem, and, for the sake of the entire staff, to provide the other with new privileges or special training. Indeed, we might have a threefold (or manifold) strategy. The consequences of a decision we envisage making may call for further decisions. These decisions can be made in stages, say as the employees develop. The decisions may also be conditional; one might decide to provide special training for a candidate *if* the person complains. Many good decisions require follow-up. The anticipation of that need may reasonably alter what one decides in the first place.

In some cases, the search for a means may also eliminate the problem, at least for a time. As we saw in exploring substantive ethical principles, considering means may lead to forswearing the end, say to deciding that no evaluation need be done for some months, which leaves time for improvement in the record and may obviate the negative review. In any case, once the conflict of obligations is resolved, we can choose the option best supported by reflective judgment (or one of a set of equally acceptable alternatives).

Universalization

A sound ethical decision should be *precedential*: it should be justifiably usable as a guiding precedent for future decisions. This is why generalization—by formulating a universally sound principle—is a good test of whether the decision is sound. Where the matter is very important or we want enhanced confidence or ability to explain the decision, it is especially appropriate to take this generalizing step beyond our decision. If we conceive our decision as precedential, we may formulate a covering principle that is rationally universalizable. Doing this might be considered a discretionary step in our model. Experienced executives, especially those who also own their businesses, may not need to proceed to it, but a *willingness* to do so and some capacity to provide at least the raw materials for a generalization are crucial. At year's end, after reviewing performance records, I may find it obvious who should be promoted. But if a colleague asks why I decided as I did, I should be willing to lay out the facts and criteria in a way that yields at least a rough principle.

Kant's Categorical Imperative (in its universalizability form) is reflected here, but we need not be Kantians to realize that if a decision is morally sound, then any relevantly similar decision must be sound and that we may be setting a precedent and may certainly have to explain or justify our decision. Consider a punitive action like levying a fine for failing to fulfill a responsibility. There might be a rule violated, a prior warning ignored, and a monetary loss to a client. If a second person errs under the very same conditions, the fine should be the same.

This universalizability principle is much like the Golden Rule: Do unto others as you would have them do unto you. But there is also a difference: Kant stressed *rational* universalizability, whereas the Golden Rule taken by itself simply refers to the agent's desires. Hence it might not yield the right results where abnormal persons (such as masochists) generalize on the basis of perverse desires.

Universalization can be especially important where a decision is made in an intuitive way *without* formulating the grounds for it. Granted, one can always say that in any case that is "like this promotion" one would do the same thing, but this similarity description is too thin to provide explanation or justification. The remedy is not to string fact after fact together in the hope of capturing the important variables in the process; it is to ascertain what is morally relevant and state that as best one can. One may still have to use such vague terms as "more productive than anyone at the same level," "loyal service over ten years," or "an inspiring team leader." But at least these factors connect with such ethical standards as justice, fidelity, and beneficence, and we know how to clarify such factors. They are also the kinds of variables that an experienced person considering promotions can consider in reviewing a record without having to articulate them in a piece of reasoning. The effort to articulate them however, and to formulate a principle governing the decision may lead to identifying relevant

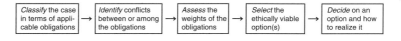

Figure 5

Five-step model for making difficult ethical decisions.

variables that were omitted. Identifying those may help one justify the decision or, sometimes, lead one to alter it.

Actual universalization, then, is not a requirement for an ethically sound decision in a case of conflicting obligations, but a kind of *universalizability* is. The effort to find a universally acceptable rule may lead to revising a decision, to carrying it out better, to formulating principles one would not have thought of that apply to the case at hand or to others, and to increased ability to communicate the basis of one's decision. All of these outcomes tend to be desirable. The proposed model might be summarized as in Figure 5.

With this decision framework before us, we should ask how it helps with policy decisions that involve *competing constituencies*, say stockholders and employees. This kind of decision is often more complicated than a difficult one involving only, say, salary for employees who report to a given manager. But the range of relevant obligations is the same (the ten described above), and the question of ascertaining and resolving conflicts will occur in a similar way. If you are Chief Executive Officer (CEO) and convinced that employees need better healthcare, how can you justify this to shareholders whose dividends may be lowered by the decision? It *may* be that a representative group of them would approve once exposed to the reasoning supporting the decision. It may be that consultation of this kind is not feasible and that you must figure out a way to do right by both these constituencies. You might, for instance, fully satisfy neither but have a rationale acceptable to both—better long-run profits for the investors, better benefits for employees. In some cases, a loan that provides more funds may be acceptable to all constituents—in this case community banks may benefit. Later chapters will indicate other respects in which this decision framework brings multiple obligations to bear on multiple constituencies.

5

ETHICAL BUSINESS, ENVIRONMENTAL RESPONSIBILITY, AND SUSTAINABILITY

We have seen that the community in which a business operates is a major constituent to which management is responsible. This includes minimizing hazards to the population and avoiding environmental degradation. One of the major ethical challenges for businesses stems from a disturbing pattern unlikely to change in the near future: growth of the world's population simultaneous with diminishing natural resources. This makes conservation of environmental potential ethically important for management, especially in companies that consume a great deal of energy or produce substantial waste or both. Even where government limits population growth, as in China, the demand for oil and other resources is increasing. The pattern we face—even in the United States, which uses more natural resources per capita than any other nation—generates special obligations.

The Value of the Environment

According to one view, the main ethical obligation arising from the pattern just described is to create technologies that reduce our dependence on diminishing natural resources. There is such an obligation, and it falls on educational institutions as well as on business. But developing such technology is not our only obligation. A partial solution to the problem is conservation. It can lower dependence on oil and reduce the pollution that harms forests and crops. This way of speaking, however, says

43

nothing about the *value* of the natural environment. What kinds of value does it have?

We have so far spoken as if the environment had mainly *instrumental value,* value as a *means* to some good, such as happiness. Instrumental value can be immensely important. Fuels have only instrumental value yet save lives. But might the natural environment also be valuable *in itself: intrinsically* valuable (inherently valuable, in another terminology[30])? It is often beautiful, for instance. On many theistic views, it is also a gift from God that deserves respect and preservation. It might also be conceived as a symbol of divine love. There are, then, both religious and other reasons to preserve the environment; not all of these are instrumental reasons.

If the environment has intrinsic value, then we should *value* (hence, care about) it as an *end,* not just as a means. Such intrinsic *valuing* is fitting for things of intrinsic *value,* much as belief is fitting to truth. But people do not always value the valuable. Just as we can believe what is false, we can value what is bad. The value system—a motivational element in us—must, like the intellect, be educated. Valuing something does not guarantee its value (its genuine worth) any more than believing something guarantees its truth.

Suppose, then, that the environment has real value and should be valued both as an end and as a means. Again, businesses may face conflicting obligations: the obligation of beneficence, for instance, might incline one *both* to drill new oil wells to facilitate transportation and, on the other hand, to avoid despoiling a beautiful but oil-rich area and thereby reducing the aesthetic value in people's lives. The decision framework proposed in Chapter 4 would help one determine the right tradeoff, such as carefully controlled, moderate drilling. But such determinations are not easy. Even when justified, they may be controversial.

The Ethical Importance of Future Generations

One of the difficult elements in determining how much exploitation of natural resources is warranted concerns future generations. People often speak of their rights, but may we ascribe rights to persons who do not exist? This is doubtful, but good ethics does not require claiming it. The principle that we are obligated not to harm persons can be justified without appeal to the rights of existing persons: it applies to doing things that will harm persons, whether they are alive at the time of action or not. The same holds for the utilitarian principle that we are to maximize well-being. Poisoning soil with nuclear wastes, for instance, harms persons if it in fact kills them, even though it cannot be *known* to kill until long after the deposits are made. This holds on any plausible ethical view.[31]

How far do such future-directed considerations go? Should we assume that humanity will survive indefinitely and that, ultimately, technological advances will compensate for depleted resources? Insofar as we take preservation of some kind of equality as a standard of conduct, and insofar as we consider justice to require equal treatment of persons, we should be guided by *a principle of intergenerational justice*: businesses and other users of natural resources have an obligation to gauge their uses so that, given reasonably expectable changes in technology and population, future generations may live as well as the present generation. This applies to governments, including utilities they control, as well as to individuals and businesses.

This principle of intergenerational justice is perfectly compatible with the view that the natural environment has intrinsic value. But the latter view may depend on a theology that many do not accept, or it may face controversy about how important aesthetic value is even if it *is* a kind of intrinsic value. The least controversial way to justify requiring preservation of the environment is ethically, in relation to justice and other human concerns. This kind of justification may be supplemented by religious, aesthetic, and other non-moral considerations; but the ethical case alone is sufficient to warrant more protection of the environment than most nations have so far enforced.

The Ideal of Sustainability

So far, the emphasis on the obligation of businesses to preserve the natural environment has been outward-looking—toward those outside the business who may be harmed or deprived by either its overuse of natural resources or its damaging the environment. But there is also an *internal* imperative supporting both conservation and intergenerational justice: sustainability.

Broadly speaking, a business or business activity (indeed any activity) may be called *sustainable* if, functioning roughly as it does, it can continue indefinitely. This generic notion of sustainability is vague in that it specifies no type of activity (such as borrowing money) or future end date. We can (and often should) be less vague by specifying both; we can say, for instance, that oil production—or gasoline consumption—*in* a given country and *at* a given rate, is sustainable only *for* a half century.[32]

Even if future generations are not in question, management should generally seek sustainability for a time that at least goes well beyond its own tenure. For one thing, many stockholders or other constituents may have long-term interests, say extending half a century. Another point is that those who have children often do not feel satisfied with a business in which they are investors unless they believe that it has a long future. Much stock is bought with the idea that it may go to the buyer's children or grandchildren.

A related but quite different point is that a managerial commitment that is not long term is unlikely to be as prudent as one that is. It will tend to reduce the confidence of many constituents, especially employees. With some exceptions, such as companies created for special projects, employees should be able to be confident that the business they spend so much of their lives serving has a long future. An employee's contribution to a sustainable company may be felt to be itself a lasting contribution—a kind of legacy—and may add significance to the sense of doing meaningful, rewarding work.

Overuse of natural resources is not the only threat to sustainability. Internal policies can also threaten it. Consider the well-known devastating fire at Malden Mills, which had manufactured a distinctive fabric. Somewhat idealistically, its principal owner compensated employees during the rebuilding at a cost he could not afford given the expenses of resuming business. Instead of finding a Confucian "middle way" or an Aristotelian mean between selfishness and lavishness, he went too far toward the latter. Beneficence was possible with less expenditure, and more good was achievable in the long run.[33]

The mission statements of prominent companies—indeed of most companies that thoughtfully compose a mission statement—often manifest an intention to achieve long-term sustainability. Businesses usually seek to have a focus and mission worth supporting. Would we want to invest in one that does not? Would banks make loans to such a company? Perhaps most important, our work in a business will not be felt to be meaningful and valuable if we cannot see it as fulfilling a valuable purpose. To be sure, purposes can be limited, such as building a bridge. But if we find meaning in working on such a project, would we not find *more* in working with a company that builds a *series* of bridges and other valuable structures? If the bridge is also beautiful and well suits its environment, the sense of meaning that accompanies the construction is enhanced.

Sustainability, then, is a source of both internal and external managerial obligations that concern both the environment and the management of a company. Sustainability is important in making work meaningful as well as in creating a legacy one can be proud of, such as contributing over time to the needs of humanity. Conservation of the environment is an aim that is ethically compelling and serves the long-term economic interests of most businesses.

6

MARKETING: PRODUCT, TARGET, AND IMAGE

Businesses do not merely supply goods and services—they market them. There are ethical and unethical ways to do this. It is ethical to distribute and publicly advertise needed products, such as household cleansers, with an honest description of what they do. It is unethical to distribute and publicly or even privately advertise dangerous and illegal products such as hallucinogenic drugs.

Some Major Dimensions of Marketing Ethics

Marketing is largely a kind of promotional representation. To see how this is so, note that wherever marketing occurs, we may identify at least five ethically significant elements: a marketer, m, offers a good or service, g, to a prospective buyer, b, for consideration, c, using promotional representation, r. These elements roughly encompass the "four Ps of marketing": product, place, promotion, and price. There are other important variables, such as the purpose(s) that underlie marketing the product and the manner in which it is made. Three further comments are needed.

First, although goods and services are the kinds of things most commonly marketed, in principle anything that can be offered and received can be marketed. One might think that only *property* can be marketed. If so, then since people cannot be property, they cannot be marketed. Given the history of slavery and the similarities between the selling of slaves and the selling of inanimate things, this restriction is at best artificial. It seems true that (apart from labor and things that cannot be property) only property *ought* to be marketed, but clearly marketers need not own

48

what they in fact market. Goods held for sale on consignment are an example. Even mere possession is enough for marketing.

Second, if only property ought to be marketed, then in recognition of the value of ideas, we must—as the law does—acknowledge *intellectual property*. This includes original papers and books, as well as plans for the production of such things as computers, vehicles, and technologies. It can be very difficult to determine *whose* property an idea or plan is. Two people can simultaneously formulate an idea, and a new design can be a slight variant on an old one. Here business ethics requires marketers to be fair in determining ownership, and users should be fair in paying for intellectual and other property.

The third point concerns not what is marketed but payment for it. Although money is normally the payment, other kinds of consideration count. One can market something for trade of a non-monetary kind, such as raw materials. Indeed, public relations firms are sometimes said to market a candidate for office. Where this is more than metaphor, monetary contributions—and votes—would count as payment for the anticipated services of the candidate.

Five Types of Ethical Problems in Marketing

If the five specified dimensions of marketing are basic, then certain important ethical problems arise. Each kind goes with a question. Consider first the *who*-question: who is doing the marketing—the chief executive officer (CEO), the marketing manager, marketing "professionals," a single individual, etc.? Second is the *what*-question: what is being marketed? Third is the *to-whom*-question: to whom is the thing marketed? Fourth is the *for-what*-question: for how much (or what consideration) is it marketed? And finally, there is the *how*-question: in what representational manner is it marketed?

In connection with the *who*-question, we should ask who is ethically responsible for marketing the product in the first place. If there is only one marketer, the answer is easy, but commonly there is a producer and someone employed to market under the producer's authority. There may even be a chain. According to a certain kind of top-down model, the main responsibility lies with the producer, say a factory owner. But others in what we might call the *marketing chain* may have considerable discretion. This implies that the producer need not be entirely responsible for what they do. Indeed, perhaps everyone in the chain, from manufacturer to marketer to distributor to salesperson, can see to it that the product goes forward., Many can also bring about its review, delay, or alteration. We might have something approaching a firing squad model, where all are responsible to a high degree, with the producer playing the role of the person who gives the order to shoot.

If, on the other hand, we take the metaphor of a chain seriously, we regard each person in the chain as capable of stopping the marketing, even if unable to control all aspects of it. Every operative link is necessary to the success of the chain, but no single one is sufficient for success. When things go badly, as where a product is harmful, the different kinds of responsibility suggested in these cases matter considerably. (There are of course other variables affecting responsibility.)

Regarding the *what*-question, there is no easy answer. Much of what people need should be marketed, but so should some things they want but do not need. It is also clear that some harmful things should not be marketed, say machine guns to the general public. But what of gambling casinos? What about Taser guns? And is it ever morally permissible to market child labor? I will return to some of these cases. But first, consider a sixth question: the *what-for* question. What is the commercial purpose of the marketing?

The *what-for* question is the one closest to the question of how what is marketed should be represented. If the only purpose is to profit, then the best selling technique possible is likely to seem necessary. But although there is nothing unethical about making a good profit, an ethical person also has both positive and negative goals of other kinds. Avoiding harm is a minimal moral constraint of any plausible ethical view. Promoting good is also important, but usually somewhat lower in priority.

The *how*-question is often answered by determining a kind of advertising. It might indeed seem that advertising is *entailed* by marketing. It is entailed by large-scale media marketing, but marketing is possible without advertising. Indeed, physicians and lawyers can market their services by communicating commercially relevant information to those they know, by manipulating their fees, and in other ways. There is, to be sure, no sharp distinction between advertising and simply spreading news or commercially relevant information. But it is surely possible to fulfill the five criteria of marketing indicated above without doing anything properly called advertising. A grower can market apples on site simply by exhibiting them with posted prices.

If marketing is promotional representation, and if its typical purpose is to sell for a profit, then, as with any kind of persuasion, there will be temptation to manipulate and even deceive. This matter needs some analysis.

Insincerity, Deception, and Manipulation in Marketing

Lying about products is commonly harmful and is always potentially so. But lying is *basically* wrong whether harmful or not (this is not to say it is never excusable, but the very need for an excuse confirms that *some* wrong has been done). That marketers should not lie is not controversial. But lying is not the only form of insincerity. This needs explanation.

Deception does not entail lying, but it is usually a kind of insincerity. Suppose we present only facts favoring our view. This is deceptive, but not lying. Another case of deception occurs with a kind of *indirect marketing*. Suppose celebrities are paid to wear a certain brand of clothing or college students judged to be trendsetters are given footwear with the idea of causing peers to want it. Such "viral" marketing may deceive, but need involve no lying. Is it objectionable, at least in cases in which wearers *pretend* to have purchased the items from natural preference? And would the latter deception—which might exhibit a kind of manipulativeness as well as insincerity—be attributable to the marketer or the wearer or both? That might depend on whether the marketer secures agreement to deceive should the question of purchase come up. Students modeling clothes and asked where they got them might or might not be truthful. Deception can, however, be innocent—as where a wig leads people to underestimate someone's age.

May we decisively judge deception to be wrong in advertising, as is lying? Consider an ad that shows someone who appears credible raving about the product and calling it "second to none." This may cause many people to think it is *better* than any competitor. But no lie is told if, though not best, it is *as* good. The same applies to showing a person who looks like a consumer preferring one's product to its competitor. This does not entail lying and, unlike denigrating a competing product, it need not imply falsehoods about that product.

To be sure, a deceptive ad may not deceive everyone. What deceives most may simply annoy a skeptic. Suppose (as a rough working assumption) that we speak of *deceptive advertising*, in the main ethically relevant sense of this phrase, when the advertising tends to produce false beliefs in normal viewers who consider it in good faith and with full attention. We may we now say that marketers should in general avoid such deceptive advertising. But it is so difficult to tell what constitutes a normal viewer or full attention that to criticize every ad that is deceptive in this sense would unreasonably burden business.

The positive point here is this: marketers should develop a consciousness of what tends to deceive and should seek ways to promote the goods or services they market without deceptive advertising. Developing the consciousness and making the effort are an ethical obligation. Occasional failure may be excusable, but a pattern of deception strongly suggests unethical conduct somewhere in the marketing chain.

Advertising and the Limits of Persuasive Representation

Advertising has enormous influence. It is greater in a given population in proportion to the reach of the media into their lives. We have already noted that a standard ethical imperative is to avoid lying and that it is possible to deceive without lying. To take a different example, suppose a product is called "unparalleled in working against headaches." This will seem to many people to claim that it is *best* in its field, and the credulous will tend to believe that. But there may be no specification of how it is unparalleled by any other medicine. Perhaps it simply works differently. Granted, deception cannot always be prevented even when one is honest and clear, since some people are too easily misled or simply mishear, or read only part of a message. But using this wording would be reprehensible if one believes there is a better competing product.

Lying and other undesirable elements, such as harming people, can explain why deception is commonly wrong. But even deception that is neither lying nor harmful is also frequently wrong; it may, for instance, be at least potentially manipulative. For these reasons, marketers should avoid deceptive advertising. The notion of the deceptive here is understood in terms of a reasonable person standard *relativized* to the intended audience. For instance, marketing a drug to physicians is one thing; marketing it to the general public is quite another. Marketing ethics requires avoiding not only lying but also advertising that is deceptive in the ways described here.

A third element to be avoided in marketing is misrepresentation; this may or may not deceive, but tends to do so. Consider ads noting what a large percentage of doctors recommend the "ingredient in Bayer." The ingredient in question (we may assume) is aspirin, acetylsalicylic acid. Assume the statement is true; still, some will be deceived by it and form false beliefs to the effect that the ingredient in question is different from the (defining) ingredient in other brands of aspirin. But, even apart from deception, the statement is arguably a misrepresentation in suggesting that the main ingredient in Bayer is distinctive.

We come now to the *to-whom* question. Clearly some things should not be marketed to children, nor should alcohol be marketed to alcoholics, say by posters outside meetings of Alcoholics Anonymous. The common-sense non-injury principle applies here. But when it comes to what is permissibly marketed to adequately informed adults in a free society, restrictions are much harder to set. What clearly causes "antisocial" behavior is ethically objectionable (even if not illegal), but what causes harm only to the buyer is another matter. Still, in a society in which taxes paid by all who have income are used for medical care and unemployment benefits, even such things as drugs that make only their users suffer directly can be ethically objectionable. They burden the public with medical or financial responsibility. This is part of the reasoning that can justify motorcycle helmet laws and could make it unethical to advertise motorcycles in a way that implies helmets are unimportant.

An even more difficult problem is how to restrict advertising from the attention of children when it is ethically inappropriate for them to be exposed to it. This apparently applies to certain violent or pornographic materials. Here we find gradations: public billboards have a captive audience and should be carefully scrutinized; what is displayed in taverns that do not admit minors is at the other end.

Regarding the *for-what* question, we have to consider fairness, especially in pricing. Unfair pricing is a case of economic injustice and may also violate the obligation of non-injury. It is perhaps not unethical to charge the maximum the market will bear if there is fair competition (a notion that is difficult to define). But even given a generally competitive environment, there can be unfair overpricing, particularly with necessities such as electricity. Unfair underpricing is also possible (in ways suggested by scenario 10 pp. 139–140).

Quite apart from unfairness, however, it may sometimes be ethically *better* for sellers to take less than the market will bear. If I can make a good profit without charging the maximum my customers will pay, then if I am selling necessities rather than luxuries I may consider myself a better citizen by not maximizing my prices. Arguably this would be *supererogatory*: not an obligation, but praiseworthy. Most ethical people want to do a goodly range of things meeting this description. As virtue ethicists stress, we all have to ask what kind of person we want to be. Supererogation goes with generosity, kindness, and compassion. I may prefer having customers go away feeling that they did well rather than simply getting a fair shake. Here it matters greatly whether my standard is virtue, including honor and generosity, or a principle calling for beneficence rather than for simply avoiding injustice and injury.

The Ethics of Creating Desire

Marketing and advertising of any kind require desire on the part of the user. But there are many kinds of desire. An important division is between need-based desire and desire not so based. But what is need? Needs are relative to some state or outcome for which they are essential. Food and shelter are needed for survival; the respect of others is needed for a good life. The second kind of need is ethically based: a good life is something there is ethical reason to seek for oneself and others—a point reflected in the obligations of self-improvement and beneficence. A good life is not just biologically based. Thus, although the *notion* of a need is relative as indicated, the *point* that people need the respect of others can be an ethical one.

Need-based desires are natural for human beings and are ethically proper targets of marketing. But whether need-based or not, desires met by marketing divide into two categories: those existing *antecedently* to marketing—especially advertising—and those *created* by it. To illustrate, a desire for a good night's sleep is need-based and antecedent to advertising; a desire for a particular kind of sleeping pill may well not be antecedent to advertising but may be (indirectly) need-based. By contrast, a desire for a powerful SUV is not, for normal persons, need-based. It may or may not be created by advertising. Is it ethical to create it and sell such products?

It would be a mistake to claim that creating and meeting desires that are not need-based is always unethical. Many things that make life enjoyable are not needed either biologically or ethically. Marketing cigarettes to minors, however, could create desires for something harmful that is not needed. One could also create desires that have *disproportionate strength*, in the ethical sense that they outweigh need-based desires that conflict with them. This would apply not only to expensive but unneeded beautiful clothes that are harmless, but also to desires for hard drugs that create a chemical dependency and are not medically needed. The desire for a powerful SUV is in not in this last category, in that it need not directly harm the user. But is the product indirectly harmful to people in general?

A strong free market view on whether SUVs are harmful would support claiming that they are not harmful in any way that warrants restriction. Some proponents of this view would hold that if pollution becomes serious enough, the free market will respond to it, since antipollution devices will become highly profitable. A counterpart argument from a welfarist perspective would be to the effect that a minimal response on behalf of society would be higher tax on purchase and use. Indeed, given sufficient environmental dangers, such as global warming (which may be irreversible), a welfarist perspective might warrant legal prohibition.[34]

The upshot is that whatever the proper tax on environmentally degrading items should be, both marketers and consumers should raise ethical questions about what they ought to do voluntarily. A manufacturer can at least *try* to make the same profits by selling something less objectionable instead or by marketing the product to a selected audience and with appropriate cautions on its use. A consumer can ask whether a fuel-efficient vehicle might serve equally well.

The Interdependence of Marketing and Manufacturing Decisions

It should be clear that marketing decisions are inseparable from manufacturing decisions or decisions on what goods and services to provide. The connection might seem to lead to the principle that what should not be marketed should not be produced. But this claim would be too strong. It would rule out currency printing (a government function) and production of certain weapons (though even then there should be at least competitive bids from industry to the military, and these may constitute a kind of limited marketing). The converse principle, however, seems sound: what should not be produced should not be marketed.

We can gain further clarity concerning marketing ethics by considering the case of the Taser gun, which uses electric shock to disable people considered dangerous. It is one thing to hold that these should be marketed to police departments, but they are also wanted by individuals for self-protection; and self-protection is a need—sometimes a pressing one even for ordinary citizens. The dangers of these guns are, however, not fully known. They may be lethal, particularly used against people with certain weaknesses or when used repeatedly. Moreover, in the wrong hands they would facilitate muggings and rapes.

One approach is utilitarian calculation. Assuming we could reasonably assign positive and negative numbers to happiness and unhappiness, we might, e.g., weigh the painful consequences of death and injury to innocent people against the benefits of more easily arresting dangerous persons and of deterring certain crimes. But ethically, it seems preferable to give the obligation of non-injury greater weight than it would have under that strategy, which would heavily weight desire-satisfaction and the feelings of security that a number of people would—rightly or wrongly—acquire by permission to use the guns. Still, the fear of attack by such weapons if they are generally available is a psychological harm that many who do not possess the weapon (and some who do) would suffer. Avoiding this fear may be more important than the positive consideration on the other side. But arguably there is a right of self-defense that would justify using these weapons. This question will likely become more prominent. At present we can conclude that, if such weapons are to be marketed, their buyers should be restricted to responsible people, and the mode of their advertising should take account of their dangers.

Advertising and the Human Image

A final point important here concerns marketing ethics as applied to advertising. A great deal of advertising requires showing people using the product or performing the service being marketed. It is natural to portray the characters who appear in such ads in a way that maximizes sales. In the United States and elsewhere the result is often to portray women (and sometimes men) largely or mainly as sex objects. Clothing ads in magazines (including some issues of the women's fashion supplement of the *New York Times*) commonly exhibit this pattern.[35] In this way, the ads may present an offensively distorted image of humanity. Are they deceptive or harmful, rather than just offensive? If not, a free society will not legally prohibit them. But from this it does not follow that the marketing of the kind of clothing (or other product) in question is ethical.

A case might be made that some ads, say of cigarettes, are deceptive or harmful or both, at least for some viewers—say children. Even when children are not the target of marketing, they may be a captive audience for it, as where they cannot help seeing ads in public buses. But consider two less controversial points that bear on marketing ethics. Recall the Kantian prohibition of treating people "merely as means." Does this not describe how many women (and some men) doing the ads might feel—or be warranted in feeling? Surely marketers should seek to avoid exploiting those who represent their products and should try to avoid using degrading images of human beings. It is not clear that doing so would significantly reduce sales.

A quite different point emerges if we shift from the marketer's to the consumer's side of marketing ethics. Consumers can express dislike of certain kinds of ads or adjust their purchasing preferences accordingly. It should not be assumed that business ethics applies only to businesses and their employees. It applies to all who do business, including consumers.

Marketing is a major element in the developed world and is increasingly global. It has not been possible to consider how marketing strategies should be adjusted for different cultures, but clearly the ethical decision framework proposed in this book can be used in that task. Marketing raises both theoretical and practical questions, and insofar as it involves advertising it raises questions concerning freedom of expression as well as of veracity, non-injury, and beneficence. These are hard questions, but it should now be clear how some of them can be ethically approached.

7

THE ETHICS OF FINANCIAL REPRESENTATION

Much as advertising is a kind of commercial representation, accounting is a kind of financial representation. Modern societies depend very heavily on it. We need good accounting even to pay our taxes. We rely on it to evaluate stocks for investment; we depend on it when we buy or sell major assets; and businesses need accounting to measure their progress. There are many technical aspects of accounting, and here we can consider only the broadest ethical standards applicable to it. Two topics will be central: the proper function of accounting in a capitalistic economy, and the ethical representation of financial status to government and the public.

The Centrality of Accounting in Capitalist Democracies

To see the importance of accounting even in simple matters, consider a contract specifying how an individual or a company will take over a business to which they have lent money if that business fails to pay its debts. A business may default on a loan while still having capable employees, money owed to it, and inventory. *Given* accounting that supports potential to turn the company around, a further loan might be obtained to avoid default. *Without* accounting to show the company's value, we cannot determine how much is being acquired as an asset by the foreclosing lender (this may be important for the lender's own profit and loss statements and for determining its tax liability). Or, suppose the company is purchased by someone who can pay off its loan. Then accounting is needed to ascertain a fair price to pay the previous owners(s). Determination of both economic value and creditworthiness, then, depends on accounting.

Even determining fair market value depends on accounting. An actual sale price need not indicate this value. A buyer may pay more (or less). Moreover, governments need a figure for fair market value to determine taxes when a business or major asset is inherited. Ethics bears on properly determining that value. Falsifying it can be cheating fellow citizens by reducing tax revenues that would benefit the public. Ethical standards do not preclude selling an asset for more than fair market value, at least *if* the purchaser has a chance to determine the value and is willing to pay the agreed price. But without accounting, there are few if any major businesses whose fair market value can be determined. Even managers who do not consider it unfair or otherwise unethical to sell things above market value may want to know whether they are in fact doing this. For one thing, it would bear on planning—in part because competitors would have an incentive to take over a company's market share by selling comparable products for less. Given fair competition, overpricing tends to lead to reduced sales, sometimes quite quickly.

A related point about the importance of accounting concerns the assessment of *people* inside a business. Consider sales. Without proper crediting of them, salespeople cannot be fairly evaluated. Crediting may or may not be simple. For instance, where one salesperson receives help from another in making a sale, how should the credit be divided? What formula is fair in figuring commissions or bonuses? The determination of such a formula is a management decision, but putting it into practice is partly an accounting problem. What information would an accountant need on sales record forms used to make a fair division of credit for shared sales?

To take a more complex case, what sorts of reports on business expenses do accountants need both for reimbursement of employees and for determining the business's tax liability? Getting the right information will be important for employees' pay and for determining the taxes of both employees and employers. Overstated business expenses tend to cheat both employers and other taxpayers. Understated expenses can waste money for both businesses and individuals. This is a case that clearly calls for a mean between excess and deficiency.

The Public Representation of Financial Positions

In a now famous case, Enron Corporation used accounting tricks—and fraud—to overstate its profitability dramatically. As a result, many thousands of people lost a great deal of money and the Arthur Andersen accounting firm, once of good reputation, went down under a cloud of legal cases and scandal.[36] Prison sentences were given to some of the perpetrators, and investigation continues regarding just who was guilty of what, but many accountants were involved in either distorting financial information or failing to stop or expose wrongdoing they suspected. In some cases, deception exploited legal means, including "special purpose entities" (SPEs), which could hide debt. These were controlled by Enron, but their debt to others—even when they had loans backed by Enron stock—did not have to be listed as a liability in Enron's accounting. The case is important not only in showing the disastrous effects of unethical accounting but also in showing that law cannot be viewed as a criterion for what is ethical. Enron is widely believed to have hidden 16 billion dollars in debt (some by legal means).[37] Legal permissibility does not entail ethical permissibility.

It is also important to consider simpler cases in which accounting ethics is crucial. The following three are common kinds of case in accounting.

Consider inventory. A business commonly has real estate, furniture, and equipment. It may also have leases. All of these must be assigned a value in order to determine the worth of a business and how profitable it is. There are generally accepted accounting standards for measuring profitability and economic value. But the standards cannot bypass judgment entirely. This enables accountants to produce a higher figure for some purposes, such as securing a loan or sale of assets or of the company itself, and a lower figure for other purposes, such as taxation on profit or land. Leases may also be represented in different ways with different tax implications, depending on whether they are treated as capital (as where they are long-term values) or as costs (given what is owed to pay for them). Accounting judgment may have to be exercised to determine the proper category.

How far should accounting judgments stretch in such cases? When does merely favorably representing a client end and cheating on taxes or inflating value for the sake of a loan begin? Plainly, to say that a business is worth approximately ten million dollars while believing it is worth nine million is to lie and is wrong. But suppose the margin of error of our method leaves an uncertainty of plus or minus $100,000. Within that range of $200,000 (between $900,000 and $1,100,000), may we use any figure we like? This depends. What precedent should we set? How would we want to be treated? Using that *self-application criterion*—which is implicit in the universalizability standard—we might want to make our best factual estimate and openly state (or at least be prepared to admit) the margin of error.

Similar kinds of issues arise in two other common domains important in accounting: depreciation and write-off of bad debt. How much does the value of an expensive machine depreciate with time and use? And when is a debt sufficiently unlikely to be paid to warrant deducting it as a loss against profits, thereby reducing tax? Again, there are generally accepted accounting standards, but there is often a need for personal judgment. This makes room for financial incentives to cause distortion of financial realities.

Judgment, Clarity, and Conflicts of Interest in Accounting

Accounting, then, is a realm where judgment weighs heavily in making representations of value, profits, or losses. Honesty, as entailing abstention from falsification and from certain kinds of deception, is essential. But there are at least two further ethical points. Sometimes ethics is compromised without dishonesty but by deficiencies in clarity or candor or both. A true and even full financial statement can be difficult to understand, for instance obscured by technical terms for all but a few readers, or fraught

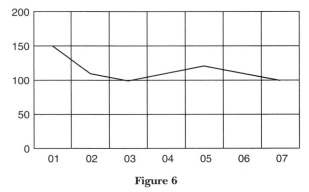

Figure 6

Graphic representation of losses, 2001–2007.

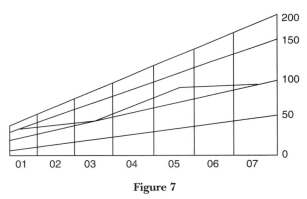

Figure 7

The same graphic pattern as in Figure 6 is misleading by being presented to look like an indication of profit.

with vague and sometimes ambiguous language. This can be an unethical evasion of the simple truth that a business has been decreasingly profitable. Hiding behind technical language can be unethical even while telling "the truth, the whole truth, and nothing but the truth."

Even without technical language one could deceive by telling nothing but the truth, yet not the *whole* truth. Consider a year in which both the company's cash position and its profits are said to rise, but only because it sells an asset at a great profit. If the profit is not attributed to normal sales (which have in fact dropped), these partial truths may deceive an unwary reader. A subtler case might occur where (1) profits are said to be improving because expenses have been reduced but (2) the reason is that, since the company is struggling to stay afloat, executives have ceased to inflate their business expenses. Someone who does not analyze the cost of making sales and the basis of the changing profit figures may overestimate the health of the business. Figures 6 and 7 illustrate how misrepresentation can occur in a way that will mislead those who, like many shareholders reading annual reports, are hasty.

The kind of candor in question in some of these cases is different from clarity, and both may be deficient because of the *manner* in which data are presented. Figure 7, then, shows how one can fulfill an obligation of matter—to report certain facts (those clearly represented in Figure 6)—while violating an obligation of manner: to do it straightforwardly and clearly. Clarity is mainly determined by how readily the material in question is understandable. Figures 8 and 9 illustrate a similar failure.

Candor is mainly a matter of giving an accurate picture of the business under discussion by providing information that, without dishonesty, could be withheld. Stating what we take to be our margin of error would be a case of candor if the margin is either not requested or we are free to say we are "unable to provide it at this time." Lack of clarity, such as we see in the distorted representations in Figures 7 and 9, may conceal or even facilitate lack of candor.

A different kind of ethical failing can occur when a person is pulled in two directions by different business (or other) demands. Suppose that as an accountant I think that a firm which is not doing well spends significantly more on accounting than it needs to and I am asked where cuts can reasonably be made. The question puts me in a *conflict-of-interest* situation: one interest is financial, with my income at stake; the other is fiduciary, with trust as advisor at stake; and these pull in opposing directions. The accountant might be able to cite several cuts not involving accounting. If management is satisfied and does not ask if other cuts might be made, the accountant would not have lied

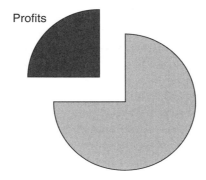

Figure 8

Standard pie chart showing profits as 25 percent of the total income for a given year.

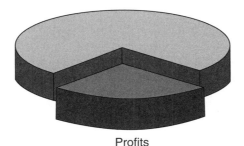

Profits

Figure 9

The same percentage as in Figure 8 misleadingly represented by a disk drawn in perspective.

and might not have even been deceptive; but not mentioning the accounting reductions would not be candid.

Conflicts of interest may also be intrinsic to *roles* or sets of roles, as opposed to single decisions. Suppose a company accountant also functions as a business consultant regarding strategic management. Strategic company decisions often involve increases or decreases in accounting needs. As consultant, an accountant might have to favor a policy that, as accountant, would be undesirable in reducing accounting profits. There is no way to prevent *all* conflicts of interest, but they should be minimized. Reducing the cases in which profit motives pull against ethics is essential to maximizing the probability of ethical conduct.

Candor in accounting and other business activities helps to expose and thereby to reduce conflicts of interest. But we should add that not everyone is *owed* candor. Casual inquiries about company finances from a non-managerial employee may deserve only minimal information. Suppose, however, that extra savings are important for the company's sustainability, and management asks the accountant for a full list of possible cuts. This would obligate the accountant to include possible reductions in accounting costs—though it might also allow pointing out additional accounting services that might save by enhancing efficiency. The point is that given the importance and complexity of accounting information, standards of clarity and candor are highly pertinent, over and above the usual obligation of veracity.

A close relative of candor, and also a virtue, is forthrightness. Consider credit card contracts. These standardly provide for loans for unpaid balances when only a portion (say ten percent of the bill) is paid on the due date. But many users do not realize something often in small print or otherwise easily missed: that the interest is charged not from the *due* date but from *purchase* dates. These may be several weeks earlier. If the interest is, say, 1.5 percent a month, this could make an immediate difference of nearly $75 on a $5,000 loan. Over time, this lending practice may greatly affect the many who buy more on credit cards than they can pay for on time. Here, as in other areas, ethical accounting and forthright financial representation are mainstays of ethical business.

PART II

The Ethics of Internal Management

8

HIRING POLICIES AND COMPENSATION STANDARDS

The different realms of business ethics are interconnected, and this book's division into parts reflects only differences of emphasis. Part I is largely about fundamentals of ethics and broad ethical questions concerning the place of business in society; this part is about managerial ethics with a largely internal focus; and Part III concerns business in a global context. This chapter addresses business ethics as a part of *employment ethics*. The latter is broader. It applies to governmental employment and employment by not-for-profit entities, such as churches and private schools. All of these, to some degree, *do* business, but they do not *constitute* businesses. This book concerns doing business of any kind, and the standards it presents apply to all business conduct, but in the interest of brevity our discussion focuses mainly on activities *in* businesses.

Preferential Hiring and Affirmative Action

In one way, all normal hiring is preferential, but business ethics is particularly concerned with preference given on the basis of characteristics that are not qualifications for the job in question. Consider selling insurance. It would be unethical to make gender a qualification. This is not to say gender can never be such; a school, for instance, might advertise for a female to be the live-in supervisor of a girl's dormitory. How might gender or any characteristic other than a normal qualification be ethically made a basis of preference?

The first thing to note is that a small privately held business has more ethical latitude than a large publicly held corporation. If you own a clothing business and you prefer female salespeople, it need not be unethical to give them preference in hiring. It would be unethical to advertise in a gender-neutral way if males are not even eligible, and it would be ethically best—and prudently candid—to indicate that some preference is given to female candidates and perhaps to say something about desired proportions of females to males, at least if asked. To be sure, if the only clothing sold is female "intimate apparel" and the clientele is conservative, being female could be a qualification for a salesperson. But let us consider employment in general and explore the notion of special treatment called "affirmative action." This has been widely practiced in both employment and admission to educational institutions, and strong sentiments favoring it are likely to keep it in effect even if the courts declare most varieties illegal.

Affirmative action (AA), in the sense most important for business ethics, is, roughly, giving some preference to members of a group identified by a characteristic not normally a qualification for doing the jobs in question.[38] Gender and ethnicity are the main cases of concern. Affirmative action comes in degrees. Here are some main types, in increasing degrees of strength:

1. Extra effort to bring the preferred group into the applicant pool, say to get females to apply;
2. Looking extra carefully at qualifications of people from a preferred group who do apply (so that, e.g., a minority person's resume that would otherwise be quickly put aside because of limited experience is read carefully);
3. Giving hiring preference when other things are *equal* in terms of qualifications;
4. Giving hiring preference when a member of a non-preferred class is perceptibly (but not substantially) better in terms of qualifications;
5. Giving hiring preference when the qualitative disparity is substantial; and
6. Giving such preference until a *quota*, such as the proportion of minority persons in the nation's (or region's) population, is matched, so long as the person hired is qualified to do the job at a minimally satisfactory level (this might, but need not, produce a great disparity in ordinary qualifications).

Rationales for Affirmative Action

Perhaps the two most important rationales for AA are that it is needed (for an indefinite time) to compensate for past discrimination and that it is necessary (again for an indefinite period) to benefit society as a whole. Consider African Americans whose ancestors were slaves and who may themselves have suffered discrimination. It may be argued that they are owed reparation, at least by government on behalf of society. As to the social benefit argument, this may be supported by utilitarian considerations, or along intuitionist lines by appeal to the obligation of beneficence together with that of self-improvement applied at the level of society as a whole. Both arguments are highly controversial, and there is a huge literature on affirmative action. It suffices here to make just a few points.

First, levels (1) and (2) AA are unlikely to be objectionable provided there is significant evidence supporting either the reparation or the social benefit rationale for AA. Policy (3) is controversial. Some white males have maintained that they lost certain jobs owing to their race or gender. Under (3), this is not strictly correct: employers might properly choose arbitrarily between equally good candidates and, apart from prejudice, would be expected to divide the jobs *evenly* over time between the two kinds of candidates. It *is* true, however, that under (3), the non-preferred candidate loses a fifty-fifty chance of getting the job—no trivial matter. Consider a representative white male. He would get only about half as many job offers in competition with equally qualified minority or female candidates. But we should quickly add that he could not complain of losing a job to someone *less* qualified. That *would* be an understandable complaint under (4) to (6).

This raises the other side of the issue: *equal opportunity* (EO). This is a kind of equality basic in both the egalitarian and libertarian democratic traditions, and people commonly claim rights to it. If rights were absolute, EO considerations would outweigh AA considerations, at least on the plausible assumption that there is not also a *right* to AA. There *is* a right of reparation for wrongdoing, but this right need not be fulfilled by employment preference.

Instead, reparations (compensations for past wrongs) might be in, say, enriched early childhood education programs, with some preference for the group owed the reparations. Still, even apart from rights to reparation, a case for some degree of AA can be made, at least in societies like the United States today—but what degree of AA, and for how long? These are difficult questions.

In hiring decisions the problem is largely one of conflicting prima facie obligations, such as obligations of reparation and beneficence that support AA and, opposing them, obligations of justice, understood as requiring equal treatment of people having equal merit. The decision model of Chapter 4 would have managers determine the strengths of these ("weighting" them) and of any other obligations in play and then consider what options there are. May managers, for instance, appoint a minority candidate who is slightly less prepared to do the job than a competing majority one? If the need to provide equal opportunity for all applicants pulls too hard to allow this, might they have preferred the minority candidate if other things were *equal* when the conflicting obligations were compared and weighted? In either case, what principle would they be using, and could it be rationally universalized?

One response is a *time-sensitive* principle, for instance one that allows preference when other things are not equal *only* until the company has a certain proportion of minority employees, say the percentage they represent among educationally qualified people in the surrounding community. There is no way that even a good decision model can make such choices easy, but the recognition of conflicting moral obligations and the need to compare their strengths is the beginning of a reasonable resolution.

If there were enough good jobs for all, the matter would be less serious (though still an important problem since, for promotions and pay, AA may compromise equal treatment). The only conclusion warranted here is that for degrees of AA beyond (3) in business, a strong case must be made in terms of past discrimination or social benefit, or both, and preferably at least one other consideration, namely the *economic argument from diversity*. This is the argument that since many businesses tend to succeed better when their workforce matches, in gender and ethnic proportionality, the population in which it operates, a carefully designed AA policy is justified for those businesses *until* they approximate this match.

The economic diversity argument is different from the *cultural argument from diversity*: since society as a whole is better off given this proportionality, AA is warranted until society approximates the match. Here the benefit is thought to be largely the "cultural value" of a mix of ethnicities at all levels of society that matches their proportion in the general population. The same kind of case can be made for *gender diversity* and, in Norway, has apparently led to a law requiring corporate boards to have a certain number of women.[39]

Opposing both arguments are two points that apparently apply to many cases of AA at level (3) or higher. First, many beneficiaries will tend to have a defensive attitude, perhaps feeling that they must justify receiving an unmerited advantage. Second, many others may stereotype beneficiaries as less competent than others and may as a result resent them.

Promotion and Remuneration

The issues raised by AA and EO in hiring decisions can also arise with promotion, salary, bonus, and, on the negative side, discipline. Managers can, for instance, use (1) to (6) in determining competitive promotions where one or more of the candidates qualify for AA. For salary and bonus given apart from promotion, managers can set aside, for minority employees, either monetary amounts or percentages of funds, say an extra one percent of salary for minority or female status. There are many schemes, and (as with hiring) employees could benefit on more than one count, for instance being both female and of minority status. They could also benefit by receiving less severe discipline for failure to perform some duty.

The idea that AA programs should not be continued indefinitely leaves open whether they should be subject to a different kind of restraint: that AA criteria should not be *reapplied after hiring*. There is a case for eliminating or at least limiting AA for persons after they are hired, especially for AA above level 3. We might distinguish between taking special steps to get an underrepresented group into the game and, on the other hand, changing the rules of play. Bringing in players not yet adequately represented in the competition is one thing; but changing the rules of the game—especially if it is a good game—is quite another. Multiple applications of AA to the same people can lead to large and alienating disparities between employees of equal or greater ability and experience. Multiple applications could, for instance, result in a minority person's being placed above one who, in terms of standard qualifications for the higher position, is quite perceptibly better. This may cause defensiveness in the former and resentment in the latter.

An important ethical conclusion that seems warranted here is that whatever the ethical case is for AA at any given level, a stronger case is needed for applications above that level, especially to the same people. One might speak here of a principle of the diminishing justification of affirmative action: other things equal, its justification is inversely proportional to the length of time it has been in effect and, for individuals, to the number of its applications to the person(s) in question. For instance, whatever the level of AA exercised in hiring someone, once that person is hired, there is (other things remaining equal) less reason, from the point of view of ethics, to give preference at the next stage, and so forth as the person continues upward. One way to see this is to conceive AA that is (1) at or above the level of giving preference other things equal, thus, robust, and (2) justified by compensatory rather than social benefit considerations as *partial compensation.* When some compensation has been paid, less is owed.

Another rough generalization that seems warranted builds on the point that the higher the level of a beneficiary of AA, the better off that person tends to be. The generalization is that, other things equal, the higher the level of such a person, the weaker the case for further AA. Indeed, a case can be made that *after* employment, normal merit criteria should take over entirely. One ground for this is that the competing candidates must work together, and harmony is best preserved—and successful business best pursued—when the criteria for promotion, salary, and bonus are geared to success in the activities in which employees are actually engaged. This point is partly ethical, but also arguable from practical and economic perspectives. A different and purely ethical point is that employees should be treated equally. This is a basic requirement of justice. It is supported by the idea that (in Kantian terms) people matter equally as ends.

Most employers also do (or should) make representations of equal treatment in salary and promotion, but they sometimes do not do so in job listings and may indeed indicate an AA policy. Some critics of AA have argued that even in hiring, it constitutes the injustice of unequal treatment. Whatever one's view on this, it should be noted that the relevant requirements of justice are not absolute. This opens the way to argue—though it does not prove—that they may be temporarily overridden by such considerations as an obligation of reparation and a need to prevent social fragmentation (which is ultimately a harm to persons). These cases of conflicting obligations are the kind we may reasonably seek to resolve using the decision framework of Chapter 4.

Qualifications and Merit

Any reasonable employment policy, including one incorporating AA, depends on conceptions of qualifications and merit. Merit incorporates qualifications, especially in hiring decisions. From the point of view of managerial decisions concerning reward—in this case promotion, salary, and bonus—what is merit? There are many criteria. Here we consider only five major (and partially overlapping) criteria standard in business.

One criterion of merit is *productivity*, in the broad sense applicable in any business. This is direct contribution to its success, whether in sales, in improved efficiency (hence higher profitability), in enhancing reputation, increasing market share, or in some combination of such variables.

A second criterion of merit is *constructive effort*, which may indirectly contribute to the variables just listed, as where an employee supports the work of others. Even taken by itself, however, effort is commonly and properly felt to call for reward or at least recognition. This may be a response to the obligation of gratitude (described in Chapter 4), even if not to that of justice.

A third criterion is *experience*, whether over a working career or in terms of time in the company. Other things being equal, experienced people are plausibly seen to merit higher compensation than those with less experience.

Fourth is *qualifications*, in the sense of the ability to do what the job calls for. This may be measured initially in terms of educational preparedness. It is correlated—though quite imperfectly—with experience, but over time it tends to be measured largely by actual performance in job-related tasks.

Fifth is *replaceability*, understood in terms of a given needed job and the supply of candidates who can fill it. This criterion has more weight the more important the job is for the business. In theory, irreplaceable employees are (financially) worth as much as the cost of losing them. The usual case is one in which there are degrees of replacement cost, and the higher this cost, the greater the (economic) value of the employee.[40]

The first three criteria are ethically important, though with perhaps decreasing moral weight: it would be unethical not to give some weight to productivity, to effort to contribute, and to experience in the job—a person's relevant history. What about qualifications—understood in terms of capacity to do the job, by contrast with actually doing it? Qualifications and replaceability are mainly practical criteria that have only an indirect connection with fairness, but they are still ethically acceptable in determining reward. Using them in determining reward is arguably required by *prudence*. Prudence is largely using practical considerations to serve one's purposes, and it would be impractical for managers to ignore an employee's qualifications or the difficulties of replacement.

Ethical standards do not provide a way to rank these criteria, say making replaceability more important than any of the others—or even outweighing all of them. Particular businesses, however, can sometimes rank them, for instance, making irreplaceability most important except for kinds of jobs that can be eliminated without major loss to the company. It is easy, however, to be mistaken in a judgment of irreplaceability—or to underestimate the difficulty of replacement.

The absence of a built-in hierarchy here is not surprising: the ten ethical principles central for the ethical decision framework proposed in this book are not hierarchical either, nor does any plausible ethical theory provide a hierarchy (including the pluralist universalism suggested in Chapter 2, which does not impose any exceptionless ordering on the justice, liberty, and happiness values central in it). Even though avoiding harm, for instance, is *often* ethically more important than doing positive good, we cannot say that *no* amount of good can offset *any* harms. At that rate, we might be unable to use chemical fertilizers or have nuclear power plants. Ethical decisions do not, however, depend on a values hierarchy. Even without it we can often see what we ought to do and frame universalizable principles to explain and justify our decisions. Universalizing can be difficult for business decisions about reward, but many managers are able to approach it using, for instance, formulas that reflect all or most of the five criteria.

Executive Compensation

It would be no exaggeration to say that in practice the replaceability criterion is a kind of free market standard of merit. Replaceability is a matter of what willing and able candidates can be found to replace someone, and at what cost. Many people tend to think that the higher up someone is in a business, the more difficult replacement would be. This is probably assumed by many who determine compensation. It is very difficult, however, to know just what replacement cost at high levels is. There is no doubt that it can sometimes be very high. It can also be exaggerated.

Recently, progressively greater concern has been expressed regarding executive compensation. The concern does not reflect any departure from the five merit criteria we have noted, but one important point is that there is a procedural deficiency in allowing executives (other than owners of a business) to play a major role in deciding their own compensation (as opposed to making reasonable demands, such as when they have a competing job offer). One result has been a move to separate the position of CEO from that of chair of the board of directors—especially where the chair carries power over (and sometimes power to choose or dismiss) directors crucial for determining the CEO's compensation. Here the term "compensation" is particularly appropriate given that many executives get much of their pay in the form of stock or options to buy it. Other forms of payment include discretionary use of corporate jets and extensive security service.

The amount of compensation of CEOs is often high enough (especially in the United States, where it is far higher than in any other country[41]) to create a sense of, if not unfairness, then special privilege at the expense of stockholders and other constituencies, especially other employees. Table 1 shows recent compensation figures for the CEOs of some major companies.

There are certain ways in which the reward criteria and ethical framework we are working with can help find an ethically appropriate way to determine CEO compensation. All five criteria apply,

Table 1

Company	Chief Executive	Total Compensation		2005 Performance of Company vs. 2004	
		Amount	Change	Net Income	Total Return
AT&T	Edward E. Whitacre	17,250,892	n/a	−18.7	+0.3
Boeing	W. James McNerney Jr.	29,763,948	n/a	+37.4	+37.8
Chevron	David J. O'Reilly	13,114,864	+30.3	+5.8	+11.4
Emerson Electric	David N. Farr	15,599,671	+166.1	+13.1	+18.9
Humana	Michael B. McCallister	5,751,248	+36.9	+10.2	+83.0
Lockheed Martin	Robert J. Stevens	9,249,046	−5.2	+44.2	+16.5
Microsoft	Steven A. Ballmer	1,009,073	+10.9	+50.0	−2.1
Sherwin-Williams	Christopher M. Connor	6,930,675	+2.0	+17.8	+3.6
Verizon Communications	Ivan G. Seidenberg	19,425,000	+15.5	−5.5	−22.1

[a]2005 compensation and change from the previous year for some CEOs of some large public companies that filed proxies for 2004 by March 31. Salary for a partial year's service has been annualized; "n/a" indicates that a two-year pay history is not available.

Source: New York Times, April 9, 2006. A table showing similar, more recent figures is provided in an article on CEO compensation for 2007, the cover story in *USA Today,* April 10, 2008, pp. 1B-3B.

but their application at higher levels of management is even more difficult than at the lower and middle levels.

To begin with, how can the contribution of a CEO be determined? One possibility is that a CEO decides to launch a new product that is plainly profitable, but commonly there is a mix of decisions with financial effect that is difficult to calculate. Moreover, even apart from this, not all company successes or failures in a given year are due even in large part to the CEO. There are market forces bigger than management. Moreover, many managerial decisions are made jointly, in which case the contribution of the CEO—or any one person—is difficult to assess.

An Approach to Fairness in CEO Compensation

Let us consider some approaches to the problem, keeping in mind that, although the criteria apply in any business, our main focus is publicly held stock companies as opposed to privately owned companies, which allow owners more flexibility. One idea inspired both by a sense of fairness and by a desire to reduce alienation among the least well paid is to establish compensation ratios. As a beginning, one could compare executive compensation to, e.g., (1) the lowest compensation in the company; (2) the average compensation in it; (3) its profitability; (4) the plight of the materially worst off in it; and (5) the "market rate" for executives at the same level.

We have already noted the problem of determining contribution to profitability and the ethical importance of considering other constituents of a business besides its executives. But even supposing we can determine approximate numerical values for all our variables, how should we choose a ratio? Here ethics gives one latitude, even though it may clearly rule out certain excesses or deficiencies, say giving the CEO a large increase (not previously promised) in a year of losses for the company and in a generally thriving industry, or the deficiency of giving no increase for several years in a row with large profits that are clearly due partly to good decisions by the CEO taken in courageous opposition to dissenters. (Consider Table 1 with these disparities in mind.) Still, ethics does not indicate any particular ratio between CEO compensation and any concrete measures of merit.

There is, however, a principle that constitutes a useful guideline. Call it *the diffusion of benefits principle*. It says that the standard for executive compensation—from the level of the CEO down—should tend to be to the advantage of all constituents, including customers as well as other employees.[42] The underlying idea is that in a free society with equality of opportunity in which all can compete for high positions, none should be alienated because of the great rewards that can go with these positions. This goal is approachable in part because these rewards may be expected to provide talented people with incentives which result in productivity that increases everyone's share of the pie. That thought—that in a free society, given EO and social mobility, one can compete to rise in status—should reduce the alienation easily caused by great socioeconomic disparities.

Since non-executive employees are the primary group that may suffer alienation, one could restrict the principle to take only or mainly them as constituents. This restriction would yield a **downward** *diffusion of benefits principle*: Only executive compensation that would perceptibly benefit non-executive employees (and here one could devise a formula for determination of adequate benefit) would be permissible. One might add that the highest priority is raising wages at the company's lowest level, at least until they make possible a certain minimum standard of living. Thus, before this point is reached, compensation benefiting only the CEO or the higher paid employees, such as the other executives, would be unacceptable. If this seems unrealistic, it should be stressed that at least one prominent CEO voluntarily did something such a plan would require: forgoing bonus money for less well-off employees.[43] But owner's rights and interests must be remembered. It would be unreasonable not to give that constituency major consideration as well in deciding compensation policies.

How would one argue that either diffusion principle is satisfied by an increase in CEO compensation? A free market argument would focus on the CEO's contribution to the well-being of the business as a whole, with special attention to such comparable cases as can be found. There might be evidence that the contribution is substantial enough to benefit all *and* that lesser compensation would, in the free market, result in losing the person to someone sufficiently less good to make even the lowest level employees (or other constituents) worse off. This kind of evidence would be very difficult to get. Ascertaining any individual's contribution to a business is often difficult, and it is often hard to determine whether a person would really leave in the face of a given disappointment in compensation. It is also usually difficult to tell how well a new person would do in the job.

Despite all these difficulties, if the criteria and cautionary points made in this chapter are kept in mind, and if the process of deciding compensation is as informed and as free of bias as possible, the results may be ethically defensible. The five criteria of merit should, moreover, be part of a company's policies. They should apply to employees upon entry and govern their expectations at later stages. This clarity about remuneration is a desirable kind of transparency.

9

CONDITIONS OF EMPLOYMENT AND CODES OF ETHICS

Chapter 8 considered hiring policies, promotion, and compensation, but we have yet to explore certain other ethically important elements of ongoing employment. These will be explored from the points of view of non-injury (roughly, avoiding harm), of beneficence, and of respect for persons, with justice as an essential element in maintaining that respect.

Safety, Risk, and Informed Consent

Among our strongest obligations are those of non-injury: to avoid injury and harm to others. These apply to managers as agents of owners as well as to individuals acting on their own. Moral responsibility, like moral rights, is *inalienable*: unlike a property right, it cannot be given away or put aside. A mining company, then, should ensure adequate safety for workers; not to do so approaches what Kantian ethics prohibits as treating people "merely as means." Similarly, sprinkler systems are generally needed in factories; chemical wastes must be handled properly; and so forth. In many countries, laws have been too lax to support ethically adequate standards. Ethics is not defined by law and demands more of us than law does or—as in dictatorships—less.

Absolute safety is not possible. How can management tell when conditions are safe *enough*? Here we can appeal to a *principle of reversibility*: by and large, if one would impartially regard an action as unacceptable toward oneself, one should not impose it on others in the same situation. (This recalls, of course, "Do unto others as you would have them do unto you.") Similarly, what we would consider acceptable for ourselves often indicates what principles we can rationally universalize.

Ethics calls for something further when conditions present significant danger, understood in terms of both the probability of being harmed and the severity of the harm in question. There must be free, informed, and adequately reflective *consent* to work under the specified conditions. Miners must, of their own free will, accept the dangers they are told they will face. Moreover, consent that does not specify *risk* is not adequately informed. They must also have time to reflect adequately on the risk. Signing a form with crucial information in fine print and with just enough time to read it once is not enough. Too many consent forms have been written with insufficient clarity or in fine print (or both), and too often they are signed without reflection.

Risk is a two-dimensional concept: there is (1) the magnitude of the harm that may occur and (2) the probability of its occurrence. Risk becomes greater with an increase in either factor. A low probability of death may still be significant; a high probability of skinned knuckles every year or so may be insignificant.[44]

Whistleblowing

Mining, construction, and other industries sometimes fail to maintain adequate safety conditions, either for workers or for products, such as tires. Here—as with wrongdoing in accounting or any other area of business—employees may face the question whether to "blow the whistle," i.e., go to authorities outside the business or to the press or some other (usually outside) person(s) in order to rectify the wrong in question or limit its effects. The decision can be very difficult. Blowing the whistle can harm other employees and even destroy the company, yet not doing so can lead to accidents or, on economic side, loss of jobs for employees and suppliers and, for stockholders, of vast sums. Employees who discover serious wrongs will likely face conflicts of obligations, at least between obligations of fidelity, say loyalty to coworkers who will be hurt by damage to the company and, on the other hand, to people, such as customers or stockholders, who will be harmed if nothing is done.

Recall the mining case. Suppose tunnels are not sufficiently secured and there is a significant chance of a cave-in—a risk that neither ethics nor the law should tolerate. A miner might first point this out to a supervisor. The ethical standard here might be called the *priority of internal resolution principle*: it says that a reasonable attempt to solve the problem should be made through internal channels if there is a significant chance this will work. But suppose nothing is done in response to making the case to one's supervisor or the person(s) closest to responsibility for the area of an observed wrong. The next question may be whether there is someone higher up in the company who may solve the problem. It might take courage to go above one's supervisor. If the miner does, the person higher up should not expose the miner or allow retaliation by the supervisor (who may deserve and receive some punishment).

What if it turns out that no one within the company is at all likely to solve the problem? This may be hard to determine, but it may be clear that the top management is corrupt or at least unwilling to correct a wrong. (This appears to have been so with Enron and WorldCom.[45]) Then the miner (or other employee) may, and perhaps ethically must, blow the whistle. This may or may not be after leaving the company. In the common relationship of "employment at will," employees are free to resign when they wish, just as employers are free to terminate the employment when they judge they should.

The case can be more difficult if the danger is less direct and the risk harder to calculate (mining experience is well documented, however, and a given miner may know of collapses in comparable cases). Or take construction. Cost cutting on materials is common. Suppose the cuts cause a deficiency in the quality or gauge of electrical wire. How much more likely is a fire given the lesser material? It may be quite unlikely in the life span of the building, which in any case will have a sprinkler system. But the risk may also be major.

Risky cost-cutting may or may not be more likely to be remedied through internal channels than by blowing the whistle on the shortcuts in construction. Many employees would let the shortcuts pass. Suppose one does. What if one then notices that the contractor is putting only half the steel rods called for in con-crete foundation materials? An engineer may know that this is serious, especially in an area subject to earthquakes. If the same engineer had let the wiring deficiency pass, there would be *greater* need to act on this second failure. A person who could be criti-cized or punished for overlooking the first violation, however, may be reluctant to act on the second. This is especially so if, as sometimes happens, blowing the whistle triggers an inquiry into the activities of the whistleblower.

This example illustrates the dangers of a "slippery slope." This commonly occurs as follows. Once a person does something wrong, even if by omission, it can be more difficult to avoid doing a more serious wrong, say as a cover-up or because the person has been compromised and feels there is now little to lose by taking the next step. The engineer who lets a wiring deficiency or a flaw in car tires pass might be told, upon initially inquiring, that the supervisor "will look into it" and might shortly afterward get an unexpected bonus that is all but transparent "hush money" yet is hard to refuse or even to accept with a warning that it will not affect the complaint. The same kind of thing can easily happen in accounting, where a false or suspicious figure is allowed to pass. A major ethical lesson here is that we must not wait until disaster looms to take an ethical stand. Damage is done on the way; integ-rity is compromised; and one can be too far down the slope to regain level ground.[46]

Healthcare Obligations and Responsibilities

There are accidents in any kind of work, and there are always non–job-related medical needs. Healthcare costs have been rising in some countries, and certainly in the United States. How should ethical businesses deal with this problem? Much depends on what services government provides. It can provide universal healthcare (even without socialized medicine), but often does not. If not, it may require employers to provide some level of insurance. But suppose it requires little or none. How should business respond?

One response is for companies to treat healthcare as a private matter and leave it to employees, perhaps paying them more than

otherwise. But employers as representatives of a group can negotiate with insurers and can usually get better coverage for employees than they could buy for themselves. Such group negotiations
are common practice, and when effectively completed—which
normally calls for employees to pay a portion if only to discour-
age unwarranted medical claims—they have the good effect of
expressing a company's concern for employees as "ends in themselves" (to use Kant's language). Where government does not
provide adequate coverage, ethical business will give high priority
to doing so itself.

Once again, we can see a difference between businesspeople,
depending on how they view the free market perspective in relation to one that favors more governmental activity or at least more
regulation. Proponents of minimal governmental interference
with business will prefer to leave healthcare for the workforce to
businesses and individuals. Others favor uniform healthcare coverage for all, at least up to a minimal level—a free democracy will
leave open purchase of private coverage leading to much more
extensive care. The former view is often supported by efficiency
arguments, the latter by egalitarian arguments. Government is
often judged to be less efficient in supplying or reimbursing for
healthcare than non-governmental suppliers. If, however, people
have equal basic rights, then, arguably, some minimal level of care
should be guaranteed by government, even if the care is provided
by the private healthcare sector.

Just what healthcare responsibilities businesses have in a
given kind of society is controversial. Here beneficence as well
as economic prosperity should figure, and employees as well as
owners are a major constituency. There is, however, one ethical
point that is largely uncontroversial: *preventive* measures should
be part of every business's healthcare program. This standard
is not met just by maintaining a high level of safety in the workplace. It concerns providing information and incentives to maintain good health. Information about the dangers of infections,
drugs, tobacco, and obesity is one element; providing information on available physicians and treatment centers is another.
IBM, for instance, has had a wellness programs for workers and
plans a program to combat childhood obesity among employees'

children.[47] Many large companies have resident medical personnel, at least a nurse or paramedic. Such people can be trained to provide advice on preventive healthcare as well as minor treatments. There are, then, many services businesses can provide beyond maintaining a safe environment. Prevention is far more economical than cure. On this point beneficence and profit-making converge.

Privacy in Employment

Both safety and healthcare in employment raise questions about privacy. A manufacturer or trucking company may require regular drug testing because of the dangers posed by drug use. It can thereby gain information that should be kept private. It may also require a medical examination for purposes of determining the possibility and cost of insurability. A psychological examination may be needed if an employee is to function well under certain stresses or is to handle dangerous chemicals. The test results should be kept confidential even if they reveal no weaknesses. Furthermore, private information should not be sought except where it is appropriately work-related. This is not a matter of simply being relevant to doing the job well, as an aptitude test might be. The collection of private information, such as psychiatric history, should be justified by a genuine need in the employment in question.

There are other needs that may limit the privacy of employees. If a business is to entrust important trade secrets ("proprietary information") to an employee, it may need to monitor some of the person's communications. Indeed, by and large, employers are entitled—provided they properly inform employees—to have access to their company e-mail accounts. Still, access is one thing; accessing is another. It is not ethical for an employer simply to indicate a right to access e-mail in case of a *reason* to exercise the right and then monitor communications constantly. If routine monitoring is the intention, the ethical thing is to indicate this and perhaps request copies of what is sent by employees over e-mail, as would be normal with paper mailings for which copies are filed.

Private Lives and the Movable Workplace

There is good reason to speak, as we are here, of privacy in *employment* rather than just in "the workplace." This is an age of the *movable workplace*. People do much from home, some jobs require little presence on a business's premises, and many employees do much of their work "on the road." Computers, company cell phones, and e-mail go with people everywhere. Some of the questions that arise concerning monitoring reappear here, but there are others.

Take the notion of "private life." If you visit a personal friend in the evening on a business trip, need your company know this? Surely not, if the evening is free and not, say, a meeting time. Suppose, however, that you are known to the public, as some businesspeople are. Then, even if the company's rights to information do not reach into a situation of private activity, business ethics may. This is a case where moral virtue makes a huge difference in conduct. People of high ethical standards consider how their conduct may reflect on their company as well as on others they care about. The public service employees do casts a positive if indirect light on their company. Drunken conduct in public has the opposite effect. It is typically not just bad ethics but bad business.

Consider also people strongly and visibly associated with a company, such as those who work in its uniform. They should try to conduct themselves in private life in a way that does not harm their company. The point does not, however, depend on wearing a uniform. An affair with a female employee recently led to the resignation of the CEO of the Boeing Corporation. In one way, it was a private matter; but even if company rules had not prohibited this kind of relationship, the behavior would not have been ethical. Let us explore why.

Company Codes and Mission Statements

This brings us to a delicate aspect of the specific rules of conduct that are appropriate to a given company. For corporations, these are an element in corporate governance, and they should reflect the ten ethical principles of Chapter 4, as applied to the specific needs and mission of the company. Assuming that the law covers much behavior in business, and leaving aside principles governing business decisions (such as promotions), what are some of the ethical principles governing personal relationships, especially romantic ones, in business settings?

Considerations of justice, non-injury, and beneficence join in supporting restraints on romantic relationships among employees who work closely in a business. The mention of closeness is needed because some companies are large enough to separate people by both distance and administrative structure, say in different cities where they are not responsible to the same managers. Some would speak of restrictions instead of restraints, but this is a realm where rigidity is unreasonable.

There is no hope of entirely preventing romantic relationships in companies that occupy a single building complex. Some of these can be between people at the same level and conducted with great discretion. A company may, however, reasonably prohibit romantic relationships between supervisors and employees whose pay or working conditions they largely determine. The former would tend to be biased in favor of—or might exploit—the latter; the latter might encounter friction with others at their own level concerned about fairness. To avoid such problems, rules might be framed so as to allow for the possibility of transfer within the company. Transfers might not always be possible, but in some cases they might reduce the kinds of problems in question.

A quite different reason for restraints concerning supervisors' workplace behavior is that an employee who is approached by a supervisor for a romantic purpose may feel pressure to respond positively. Some kinds of pressure rise to sexual harassment and, as violations of the non-injury principle, are wrong. But even friendly approaches from a supervisor or other coworker may compromise an employee's freedom. For similar reasons, a *strict principle* would prohibit romantic relations between people of substantially different power in the company. A *moderate principle* might make exceptions for people separated enough in their work to minimize the chance of abuse of power, such as the higher-level person's communicating (whether positively or negatively) with a supervisor of the lower-level person.

Many other principles and standards may be formulated concerning personal conduct in employment contexts. To some extent, such standards are implicit in many codes of ethics, in such notions as professional conduct, mutual respect, and—to use a favorite term in business ethics—"integrity." Those terms provide no clear direction, but neither a code of ethics nor a mission statement can explicitly cover every kind of case that demands ethical judgment.[48] Still, guided by managers who explain and live up to it, an ethics code can have a highly positive effect. In any event, a code cannot be well constructed without reflection on the cases it is to cover and the rationale for judging them.

More generally, a company's ethics code should be an application of ethical principles to the environment, culture, and purposes of the company. Its purposes and ideals should be expressed in a mission statement, and—even if they are largely unwritten, as with some small private businesses—its ethics code and its mission should be complementary. The ten ethical principles proposed in Chapter 4 (and similar general moral principles) are a good basis to guide composition of codes and mission statements, and they are more specific than the general standards provided by Kant's Categorical Imperative, by an overarching utilitarian principle, or by calls to cultivate moral virtues. The principles do not dictate the content of an ethics code, but a good code should be harmonious with and reflect them, with added elements to address the particular business in question. Integrity in business and, more generally, ethics in conduct, cannot be dictated in detail by a code. But a good code, reflecting the ten principles stressed in Chapter 4 and integrated with a good mission statement, can do much to reinforce ethics in the conduct of business.

10

RELIGION IN THE WORKPLACE

Freedom of religion is a central element in free democracies, and religious commitments should not be expected to be checked at the door of the workplace. Most business environments, however, are not appropriate places for audible or visible religious observances. In addition, religious differences among employees may create tensions if such observances become prominent in business settings. Secular workers may dislike any such observances; religious workers may dislike the observances of others. What ethical standards should guide management and employees in relation to religion?

Church–State Separation as a Starting Point in Employment

Insofar as businesses may be conceived as *governing* their employees, their management practices may be illuminated by the best theories of the relation between church—meaning religious institutions—and state. This starting point may be uncontroversial: free democracies should maintain some separation of church and state.[49] In broad terms, government officials should not interfere in religious education or church governance, and (perhaps controversially) clergy—in their *official* capacities—should exercise restraint regarding political activities.

Businesses, however large, are not governments, but three principles important for any democracy may also apply to management practices in both business and government employment. These three principles have legal backing in the United States and many other countries, but they can be viewed as broadly ethical principles.[50] The first principle expresses the kind of commitment to freedom that is central in the U.S. Constitution. Call it *the liberty principle*: Government must protect religious freedom. The second church–state principle affirms a kind of evenhandedness. Call this *the equality principle*. Government must treat different religious institutions and groups equally. In part, the rationale for this is to protect freedom (including freedom of religion). Governmental favoritism toward any one religion tends to give its institutions and followers sociopolitical power that may abridge the freedom of others (as where clergy have power to pass laws restricting religious expression). The third church–state principle is *the neutrality principle*. Government must not prefer religious institutions, or religious citizens, *as such* over non-religious ones.

The force of "as such" is to allow for differential attention to a given religion, if only because it needs either more protection or, say for public health reasons, more restriction. Suppose, for instance, that a religious group objected to inoculations or to drug testing that requires drawing blood. An employer—especially but not necessarily a government one—able to justify requiring these on health or safety grounds does not violate the neutrality principle. Absolute neutrality is not a requirement, as shown by the legitimacy of ordering inoculations. Neutrality requirements are, however, imposed equally on the religious and the non-religious and for the benefit of all.

If religious freedom includes freedom *toward* religion itself and not simply freedom to choose *among* religions, then the rationale for the liberty and equality principles supports the neutrality principle. That may also be seen as an equal protection principle: it implies that governments are to protect the rights, especially the freedom rights, of the non-religious as much as the rights of the religious. A related rationale—also applicable in business and other employment—concerns interests. If a democracy is of, by, and for the people, then (at least at the constitutional level) interests of the non-religious should be weighed equally with those of the religious.

Some Applications to Managerial Policy Questions

Any well-ordered business has much in common with a government. First, it is rule-governed, even if loosely; second, depending on (among other things) how readily employees can find alternative jobs, it may have coercive power over them. One major concern of ethics is what constitutes a fair system of rules; another is how to limit coercive power. On both counts, employment practices in business raise some of the same ethical concerns as government employment. Moreover, we have seen the rise of multinational companies whose wealth exceeds that of many nations. The multinational character of many businesses makes the question of religion in the workplace even more important.

In the case of private employers, the analogy to government is matched—and in some ways counterbalanced—by the analogy to an individual citizen. Indeed, businesses are sometimes owned by a single individual. Even when they are not individually owned, the liberty guaranteed to free associations extends to them. Let us first consider private businesses that do not have publicly traded shares, especially those that are "closely held," say by one nuclear family. A plausible ethical point here—a *standard of managerial discretion*—is *the private business standard regarding religion in the workplace*: privately held business, such as some selling religious books or artifacts, may give some preference to religious persons. These businesses are not, then, unqualifiedly governed by the equality principle—and this is largely because they *are* protected by the liberty principle.

Is the degree or kind of religious preference permissible in private business ethically limited at all? The degree may be high, but ethics does not allow businesses unlimited preference for a religious group, irrespective of competence, character, gender, or other variables important for the success of the business and the well-being of society. Nondiscrimination of certain kinds is a moral obligation of businesses that operate in free democracies. Even if they do give preference to a given religion (perhaps that of the owners), they should not discriminate on the basis of sex within that group or disadvantage employees who pursue—within morally acceptable limits—another religion.

There are, then, differences between businesses and governments as committed to the liberty, equality, and neutrality principles. For whereas a free democracy (1) may not prefer one religion over another and (2) may not even prefer the religious as such over the non-religious, these limitations do not apply to companies. Ethics allows them—within limits and given openness regarding the operation of the policy—to prefer even a *particular* denomination in hiring and promotion. These limits are difficult to describe. It is one thing for owners of a company to prefer, say, a candidate for employment who shares their religion; it is another to do so when someone religiously different is far better qualified for the job in question.

An *employer* need not be a *business*, but government employers such as the U.S. Postal Service compete with businesses, and whether they are viewed as businesses or not, they must operate under management policies that take account of religion. The policies appropriate from an ethical point of view vary widely, but a reasonable *principle of managerial restraint* is *the governmental employer principle regarding religion in the workplace*: governmental employers should adopt management policies that accord with the liberty, equality, and neutrality principles.

Religion in Large Public Companies

We have so far not considered very large, publicly traded companies, such as GE, IBM, and Merck. Such companies are legal persons, but because of their size, the diversity of their workforce, and the impersonal relation of most of their stockholders to management, the appropriate ethical standards for their treatment of religion are less permissive than those for closely held companies. For publicly held companies (with special exceptions), management should follow *the default principle regarding religion in the workplace*: Abide by policies toward religion that conform to the liberty, equality, and neutrality principles.

This default principle admits exceptions. There may be adequate reason for departures from it and for policies more like those of certain privately held businesses. Even a large, publicly traded company is owned by its stockholders, who, by virtue of ownership, have special rights and may in special cases ask for a certain policy. If, for instance, enough stockholders of Target Corporation wanted to reinstate the canceled policy of allowing the Salvation Army (which is religiously affiliated) to ring bells and solicit contributions, this would give management good reason to allow it. Even apart from such stockholder initiatives, a large company might consider a non-denominational chaplaincy to provide support for employees whose religious or spiritual needs might be partially met by having such a person available for consultation or, in special cases, religious services in an appropriate place.

Like any company, a large publicly held one also has special responsibilities toward its employees. In determining policies toward religion, as in certain other important matters,[51] it is appropriate for management to consult stockholders as well as employees. This may be done in various ways. Given the technological resources of many companies, electronic communication is likely to open up new opportunities. In any case, it is reasonable for directors who are elected by stockholders to address management's position on religion in the workplace. This may often center on affirming a nondiscrimination policy as regards religious applicants and employees; but neutrality may be included as a standard by adding the non-religious to the description of the groups with respect to which there is to be no discrimination.

Quite apart from such formal procedures, management at any level can exercise judgment as to what is appropriate for the company in relation to religion. Such judgment should take account of several important variables. One is the composition and apparent preferences of employees. Another is the preferences, so far as they can be determined, of stockholders. Still another variable is how well a standard fits the company's mission statement and ethics code.[52] There may also be differences in the kind of policy regarding religion followed in different phases of the business, say in restricting observances by employees as opposed to customers. Businesses cannot set rules for their customers' behavior, even on company premises, to the extent that they can for their employees.

Demonstrative Affiliation in Employment

Given the guiding principles now set out, we might look at a problem that enables us to see quite concretely some issues facing business today. Consider *demonstrative affiliation*, that is, public indication of religious affiliation or religious belief. This may be exhibited by businesses or by individuals. Particularly in a pluralistic society, it may have divisive effects. In some places, prominently wearing a cross or the Star of David could be divisive; in many places, burkas or headscarves, as required of women in certain Muslim denominations, may be so.

Should there, then, be dress codes prohibiting sartorial demonstrative affiliation? The liberty principle implies that religiously demonstrative dress is permissible. There are, however, exceptions. In many employment contexts, dress codes that may restrain religious expression are ethically permissible. Indeed, where restrictions are sufficiently work-related (as where safety in operating machines is at stake), dress codes may be desirable. But in a free society restrictions on religious expression should be carefully measured, and sartorial standards required by a worker's religion should have a special—though not sacrosanct—place. Wearing a cross or Star of David on a chain seems a minimal freedom. Wearing a head scarf indoors is more prominent; wearing T-shirts covered with boldly displayed scriptural injunctions would be another matter and, in many businesses, objectionable. In most cases, neither the prohibitions of Leviticus nor the permissions of Nietzsche should be worn on T-shirts on company premises.

Demonstrative affiliation goes well beyond clothing. Consider visible praying. Or take acts likely to be intrusive: preaching, proselytizing, or prominent self-description during working hours and in a context in which it is gratuitous. These are only some among many other ways of manifesting a religious affiliation. What limited generalizations may we draw?

One point has been suggested: a privately held company may in a limited way "establish" a religion, but must do so without certain kinds of discrimination. For instance, even where ethics allows employers to prefer people of a certain religion as employees, it does not license discriminating against some of these on the basis of race or ethnicity. Perhaps we may affirm a *limited establishment standard for privately held business*: Management in such a business may give preference to a particular religion provided (1) the strength of the preference is not disproportionate to that of the preference of the owners and (2) the preference is not in itself ethically objectionable, as would be favoritism of those who advocate subordinating women or kill civilians for political ends.

We can again see both liberty and equality—hence both democratic traditions—reflected in the managerial ethics toward religion. Employees should be given as much freedom as is consistent with the harmony, success, and ethical standards of the business, and their religious practices and convictions should be treated, as far as possible, equally. Neutrality toward religion extends this egalitarian stance toward the non-religious, who are a very large group in advanced societies today. As in other matters of conduct in employment, privately held businesses have more latitude than publicly held ones. But respect both for religious employees as such and for the non-religious requires balance and discretion in providing for free exercise of religion, whether in observances, demonstrative affiliation, excused absences, holiday celebrations, or other forms of expression.

11

MANAGERIAL LEADERSHIP AND
CORPORATE CULTURE

The subject of religion in employment, like that of privacy and
many other topics in business, shows that ethics requires judgments that are not matters of interpreting law or even of applying
established moral principles, such as those an ethics code might
list. Decisions in these areas are challenges to ethical leadership.
There is no doubt, however, that the higher the ethical level intrinsic to the culture of a company, the less often managers have to
make difficult ethical judgments on the conduct of employees or
on the policies of the company. Ethics can and should be *internalized*. Ideally, its standards guide us from inside, often spontaneously. In general, if a businessperson has to think about whether
to lie, whether to keep a promise to a client, whether to treat
males and females equally, or whether to give credit to someone
else for a good idea when the person is being evaluated, something is seriously wrong.

Corporate Culture, Ethos, and Ethics

No business is too small to have a culture, but ethical scrutiny of
culture in business is most urgent in large companies. The culture
of a company is manifested not just in what is admired in it, but also
in what is laughed at. These patterns are strands in a major element
of corporate culture: its *ethos*. The ethos of a group is (roughly)
its *prevailing* standards of acceptable behavior. The prevailing standards of a group are those actually adhered to by a suitably large
proportion, normally a majority. It need not be all; dissenters may
exist and, in some cases, be comfortably accommodated.

Why isn't ethos equivalent to ethics? The notion of ethos is sociological and concerns de facto patterns: what *is*, rather than what *ought* to be. A corrupt society (like that of the Nazis) may have an ethos, but, being grossly immoral, little or no ethics. Ethics, then (in the normative, prescriptive sense in question) is a comprehensive set of sound standards of right and wrong.

To recall an earlier distinction, the ethos of a company is determined by what is *valued* in it, but ethics—which may or may not be part of its ethos—is largely a matter of what is in fact (morally) *valuable* or, in persons, of actually respecting what is valuable. The range of the valuable is recognized by the ten common-sense intuitive principles stressed in this book and by its pluralist universalism as an integration of them, but sound ethical principles may also include (among other standards) certain Kantian, virtue-ethical, and utilitarian standards.[53]

Ethics can and should be internalized, and the ethos of a company can incorporate ethics. Ethos tends, however, to include elements not belonging to ethics. Where ethics allows coworkers to compete in fair and friendly ways, the ethos of a company may go against this. For instance, ruthless competition may be usual. By contrast, given a communitarian ethos, *teamwork*, with members taking little personal credit for success, may be the preferred norm and may be enforced by social pressure. Deviation from the ethos—say, a curt but not unethical dismissal of intrusive questions from a client—need not be met, as unethical behavior often is, with "That was wrong." The response might instead be, "This is not our way." Ethical standards, then, need not encompass a company's entire ethos.

Does a company's ethos encompass all of its corporate culture? It does not: corporate culture goes beyond ethos and may be in some tension with it. For one thing, corporate culture is determined in part by the style of corporate governance.[54] Is it top-down or more consultative or even, on some issues, democratic? Many think that democratic government is the only kind that fully recognizes human dignity. They may therefore press for an ethics—and culture—of business in which those with authority try to derive it as much as possible from the community as a whole or at least from their own "team."

Consultative and democratic styles of management can be very effective, and many workers are motivated by being asked for input. Even when it is clear *what* decision should be made, the *way* it is made and communicated may be crucial for its success. Determining mode of governance and communication is in part a matter of practical decision. We should remember that there are obligations of *manner* as well as of matter, and in many cases ethics will constrain the *how* of managerial conduct as well as its content.

A related aspect of corporate culture and governance is *transparency*. Transparency is determined (roughly) by how much of what goes on in a company, particularly decision making, can be seen by those properly concerned with the company, above all employees, shareholders, and analysts who make recommendations crucial for assessment of the business or its stock.[55] Degree of transparency is an element in a corporate culture; some cultures are open, some closed. But, especially where openness is minimal, transparency need not be a part of its ethos or called for by its ethics code or its understanding of ethics.

Even when extensive, transparency is not indiscriminate. It does not prevent maintaining confidences where they are appropriate, as in medical records, nor does it imply broadcasting corporate decisions. It is more a matter of what can be seen or determined by appropriate observers, not of what is publicized.

Still another element of corporate culture is the *atmosphere* of the workplace: its degree of formality in interpersonal relations and dress, its humor or lack of it, its pattern of socializing. How easy is communication with one's boss? Is humor used to avoid embarrassment over mistakes or in correcting people's approach? Do people lunch together or escape to the outside world—or stay glued to their workspace because of competitive pressure? Do they sometimes meet just as friends after hours? Corporate culture can be almost as much a result of its seasonings as of such basic ingredients as personalities, products, and rules of conduct.

Good ethics should be part of a company's ethos; an ethically based ethos should be the constitutive core of corporate culture; and corporate culture should be both supportive of the company's mission and leavened by beneficence and a respect for employees as individuals. This threefold statement expresses a major standard of business ethics, but it is probably not controversial. Its meaning for a given company, however, may well be controversial. How to realize the standard it expresses is not always clear, nor is there always one best way.

Managerial Hierarchy and Its Limitations

In one picture of corporate leadership, it is both *top-down* and *hierarchical*. Top-down corporate leadership occurs when the top person, typically the CEO, exercises leadership that provides definite direction to those below (though there may be more than one top person, as with the Gallo Winery, which has had co-presidents). The CEO may, for instance, get those below to implement policies that can be implemented at their levels. Some managerial influence, to be sure, is a matter of *role-modeling* and occurs independently of what specific policies or activities the CEO (or any executive) articulates or promotes.

Hierarchical leadership need not imply such a top-down structure. Such leadership occurs when management at each level has direct authority over the level below, but it allows that once policy comes to managers from above, they have autonomy. The CEO is above the sales manager, for instance, but need not interfere with the sales force, and the sales manager need not interfere with managers of local franchise dealers. Hierarchy, then, can permit much *delegation*. Prudent delegation inspires innovation, builds confidence and competence in those given major tasks, and respects freedom in those charged with responsibilities.

Good leadership can be top-down, and hierarchical patterns of one kind or another are common in business. Top-down leadership provides an incentive for a CEO to have a strong ethical influence on corporate culture, but a more consultative or even a qualifiedly democratic style can also provide good opportunities for CEOs and other executives to have a positive effect on corporate culture. Here, as with ethics generally, what one does may have much greater influence than what one says. *How* one does the things one does is also ethically important. A negative performance report can be given constructively or sharply, dryly or compassionately. The style of leadership is not fully separable from its substance.[56]

Leadership Versus Power

Leadership requires a measure of power. But power, unlike leadership, can be exercised unobserved from behind the scenes. Leadership requires contact with those to be led. Indeed, good leaders *empower* others. They generate enthusiasm and show how things can be done. Perhaps the best way to empower and motivate others is to inspire their inventiveness and reward their successes. This is often best done by allowing all who are capable of it to exercise leadership in respect to their own work. Can someone develop a special sales technique, a faster way to assemble computers, an improved design in software? Power can force compliance, but leadership inspires loyalty.

Managers need the authority to intervene, but good leadership makes frequent intervention unnecessary and allows delegating significant tasks in which employees can exercise leadership themselves. Intervention reduces freedom; consultative management and limited hierarchy give freedom more scope and may express respect for persons. Some hierarchy is desirable, however, in that without it there can be unclarity about who is ultimately responsible for a given range of activities, say those in marketing or in benefits policy. But ethics calls on managers both to minimize rigidity in hierarchy and, especially with highly trained employees, to enhance freedom and respect for persons. Managerial leaders can achieve this in very different ways, from top-down governance to participatory role modeling. The latter was exemplified by JetBlue's David Neeleman: "When other airline CEOs were raising ticket prices, wringing concessions out of shell-shocked unions, and begging the government for loans, David was issuing boarding passes, loading luggage, and handing out biscotti to grateful customers…a powerful message to JetBlue employees: what they're doing is important."[57]

In this chapter and earlier ones we have seen differences that have been described in terms of a contrast between *transactional* and *transformational* leadership. The former is largely a matter of getting business plans and policies efficiently realized, and it goes well with hierarchical, even authoritarian, management. The latter is largely a matter of changing employees' values so that they "buy into" the company and spontaneously pursue its policies. The contrast is not sharp, and both kinds of leadership come in degrees. Moreover, in certain cases some degree of each is desirable.[58]

Some managers are temperamentally transactional, but many great business leaders have been able to transform employee's values in at least some respects. This can be carried too far, as it has been in totalitarian societies developing military industries. There is also a danger of exaggerating the desire to beat the competition; the result can obscure the standards of ethics and quality that honest businesses should have.

To see how transformational leadership may be a positive good, recall what we saw in considering how marketing may ethically create desires. Values, like desires, may or may not be need-based, and values that are not—at least not economically need-based—may be ethically admirable. A pharmaceutical company could evoke altruistic values that support curing the sick. Seeking excellence here is a worthy goal and is distinct from that of being first in sales of new drugs whether or not they are the best one could manufacture. In this industry as in many others, an employee who begins work in order to prosper economically can learn to value far more—and may as a result have a richer life.

Ethical Leadership and Leadership in Ethics

Our discussion has focused mainly on managerial contexts, but *anyone* can be a leader for *someone* in relation to *something*. The lowest-level employee may be a good leader to a person newly hired—or exhibit leadership in negotiating, say, a division of responsibility among peers that is a model of compromise from which managers can learn. We have also seen many ways in which ethical standards should inform leadership. But the best leadership is not just ethical, not even just ethical and also effective from a business point of view. The best leadership also *engages* ethics. It manifests some measure of leadership *in ethics*.

One might think that ethical leadership would be best manifested by designating someone for the role, for instance an "ethics officer." Some companies have an ethics officer. Ethics officers may or may not have another title, say "Vice-President for Human Resources."[59] The specialized knowledge of such a person can add significantly to the ethical element in the company's culture, but this effect is not automatic. Indeed, it is often stressed that the CEO must play a leadership role in creating a good company culture, but people at all levels can contribute.

Large companies often have compliance officers, who may also double as ethics officers. But compliance officers are usually attorneys. Their concern is more with meeting legal demands than with promoting ethical standards that require more than operating within the law. Compliance with the law, like acting within our rights, is not sufficient to meet high ethical standards.[60]

In the light of what has been said about ethical leadership, it will be apparent that such leadership is not fully realized without what we have seen to be something more: leadership in ethics. Granted, in domains that—unlike the governance of large corporations—do not call for complex moral decisions or subtle moral reasoning, leadership can be ethical without exhibiting the criteria for its success in the way we would expect from leadership *in* ethics. But there is *room* for leadership in ethics in any walk of life. Like managers and even CEOs, rank-and-file workers in (for instance) manufacturing or in entry-level retail sales can be not only highly ethical but can also *address* ethics in the way required for leadership *in* ethics. Ethics mandates its own appearance. Everyone—and especially leaders—should not only live it, but also show it.

These points may appear to imply that ethical leadership is equivalent to leadership that clearly conforms to the ten ethical principles articulated in Chapter 4. A case might be made for that view. But it is misleading to make the case negatively, by taking ethics to require mere non-violation of ethical standards. Some of the principles express highly positive goals. Consider the obligation of beneficence. Even when we do good deeds only to the obligatory degree, say create a basically safe working environment, ethical ideals call on us to do more if we can. There is no precise answer to the question of how much this is.

It is characteristic of morality to demand that we ask, at appropriate points, whether we are doing enough. Consider the indefinitely demanding goal of beneficence. There are *ideals* of beneficence; these can be achieved only by supererogation—going beyond just fulfilling our obligations. An ethical leader not only avoids being unethical but seeks to fulfill certain ideals that call for positive conduct that exceeds the requirements of duty. This point is supported by studies of highly ethical leaders[61] and comports well with the charitable role that many companies try to play. Granted, giving to charity may be good business (profitable), but many business leaders support the practice for independent reasons.

We can distinguish, then, between leadership that is simply ethically adequate and leadership that is truly admirable from the moral point of view. Whatever one says about this difference, it is probably uncontroversial that—both for the welfare of those led and from the moral point of view—it is best for leaders to be not just ethically in the clear but also morally admirable. Stressing that point can be motivating to leaders in business and in other walks of life. Virtue and ideals have an attractive power that should not be weakened by conceiving ethics as stating only constraints or only the standards society has a *right* to demand leaders meet.

Meaningful Work and the Creation of Value

Leadership in ethics, as distinct from ethical leadership that does not rise to this, is commonly (and always potentially) a major element in what has been called "leadership as meaning-making." Actions in an organization are sometimes called *meaningful* when their "undertaking (1) supports some ultimate end that the individual personally values and (2) affirms the individual's connection to the community of which he or she is a part."[62] Leadership in ethics stresses ultimate values such as justice, fidelity, and the well-being of individuals—the object of the obligation of beneficence. Clearly these values are interpersonal and support a sense of community among those who internalize them. Prominently stressing that *we*—the company's workers—are to be guided by such other-regarding values may be expected to reinforce both the sense that the shared work has meaning and the felt interconnection among those charged by their leaders to act within the structure those values provide.

The point, then, is not that meaning in work is literally made by leaders. But leaders can do much to make work meaningful in the ways just described. Similar points apply to what is called the "creation of value." There are two kinds of value in question: valuing, which is subjective, and value as genuine worth, which is not. We can help people to value what really has value. This is like helping them to believe what is true. We can also create things that *have* value. In a way this is creating value, since there will more in the world that *has* value. A distinctive role of leadership is to determine what kinds of things really do have value and how to create them. Sometimes "creating value" is used to describe making money. There is nothing wrong with making money, but it is a mistake to think it has *basic* value. It is a means to certain things of basic value, but not properly valued for its own sake.

Leadership, then, is a basic element in the ethos and corporate culture of a company. It can ethically influence them in highly positive ways, whether or not it is top-down and regardless of its degree of hierarchy. But it succeeds best when it is not only ethical—as where it reveals internalization of sound moral principles and adherence to a good corporate ethics code—but also exhibits leadership in ethics: addressing and modeling ethical standards in both the content of decisions and the manner of their execution.

PART III

Ethical Problems of
Global Business

12

INTERNATIONAL TRADE AND CROSS-CULTURAL STANDARDS

This is an age of multinational companies, operating in more than one country, often in many, and frequently in areas that differ greatly from one another in language and culture. How should business ethics take into account the challenges brought by cultural, legal, and economic differences? There will be overlap between the ethical standards prevalent in different countries—largely because there are universal standards—but there are also differences arising from special circumstances.

Intercultural Understanding

Differences in language can be a serious obstacle to doing business. Even where, as in most of the world, at least some English serves for basic communication, delicate negotiations, direction of workers, and sometimes simple courtesy require a good understanding of the language native to the main businesspeople one must work with. The respect for persons that ethics demands calls for special efforts by businesses to have some employees learn a foreign language important to the company, to have good translators available, and to exercise special care in understanding unfamiliar customs. But even good translations can be misleading, and some customs may be difficult to discover without consulting a native. A mere seating arrangement at a business meeting can offend. Declining food one does not like may require deftness. Foreign names should be pronounced correctly within the limits of one's native language.[63]

Both respect for others and effective business may require extending latitude toward foreign employees. But how much latitude? We should not apply "When in Rome do as the Romans do" to all cases. We have seen, however, that religion is a special case. In an Islamic country, for instance, many workers will seek time to pray, and this may interrupt certain projects. Allowances should be made so far as possible. Apart from safety considerations that dictate otherwise, moreover, Muslim women should generally be allowed to wear burkas. Management might also allow leaves with pay for certain religious holidays.

Respect for other cultures and for religion does not, however, require compromising sound ethical standards. Consider an authoritarian society like that of China. Much controversy has arisen since 2006 over the apparently unwarranted concessions made by U.S. Internet companies in order to operate in China. On some accounts, the access to Internet records which the Chinese government acquired enabled it to trace and prosecute dissidents whose rights were thereby violated. This kind of case illustrates how we might feel pressure to compromise ethics in order to do business in a certain country. By way of balance, it should be noted that one might (as utilitarians would) calculate the tradeoffs to try to ensure that the advantages for freedom and justice of doing business as required offset the bad effects of one's compromises. An Internet company might argue that access to vast quantities of information about the world outside authoritarian societies tends to weaken their control of the people.

One other case should be mentioned: the position of women in many countries. Equal treatment of women is a demand of justice, but it is sometimes inadequately achieved even in countries where the law requires it. It is certainly not achieved universally. The problem is more difficult than simply providing equal pay for the same work; it is more acute when it involves giving women positions of authority over men, particularly men formerly at the same level. A transfer can help with the latter problem, but may not be possible. Here management must seek diplomatic ways to achieve justice with minimal conflict.

Child Labor

In many parts of the world, child labor is common. It has even included (in parts of Africa, for example) mining. Because of their needs and great vulnerability, children should have special treatment. Partly for this reason, an international business may decide never to employ children. Does ethics require this policy? Let us first consider children under fifteen.

It is easy to think that children under fifteen must be in school and not employed, especially in manufacturing. But in some countries many children might be unable to afford schooling past a much earlier age and would in any case need to work during other times to keep themselves and their families supplied with food and shelter. A simple prohibition of employing children under fifteen is unnecessarily rigid. Still, doing so, except on a part-time basis, is undesirable.

Suppose we now consider children under twelve, since many of them are even now employed for substantial number of weekly hours. For these children the practice is in general ethically objectionable. But that point does not settle the matter. We should again note the importance of the facts of the case. What would happen to them or their families if they did *not* work significantly long hours? It might be starvation. And what kind of work is in question? Suppose the work is not harmful. And suppose that the employer provides certain benefits, such as supervised recreation and education.

The use of children in the Brazilian shoe industry has been much discussed. Let us consider that. Suppose that poverty (not parental greed, say) is what necessitates it, and that dangerous glues and other chemical hazards can be eliminated and good working conditions provided, with adequate temperature, lighting, and plumbing. Suppose, too, that the hours per week allow attending school part time, that there is supervised recreation, and that one hour per day is given to special instruction. This would add to the cost of the shoes, but might still allow a good profit. We might now think that employing children within these standards, though undesirable, is minimally permissible until economic conditions are improved.

To be sure, the conditions that lead to child labor should be fought. But until much progress is made there will be parts of the world where at least teenage children must work for much of the week to maintain themselves and their families. If a company either employs children or even does business with those who do, it should take major steps to protect the children from harm and to support their education. The aim should be to achieve at least a good reading level, basic math skills, and the kind of applied knowledge that carries good prospects of employment.

Gift Giving in Business

A difficult question of business ethics concerns gifts and bribery. Bribes and certain kinds of gifts can be unethical in any society— on the part of both givers and receivers. But bribes and seductive "gifts" are acceptable in the ethos of some societies where multinationals do business, and they present a problem for companies that—quite properly—consider them unethical. Gifts and bribes are treated together here because, from many of the former, there is a "slippery slope" to the latter.

Gift giving is a common expression of goodwill, and in some societies businesspeople might offend by refusing gifts, at least if they cannot say that company rules prohibit accepting it. What is wrong with accepting a leather wallet or even tickets to a sports event? This depends. How difficult are these tickets to obtain? If they are hard to get, why would a business associate give them to you except to influence you? Again, it depends. If the mutual business activity is completed when the gift is offered and no other business is in prospect, this tends to lift suspicion. Otherwise it may not.

Suppose you are offered an expensive set of golf clubs with no strings attached. May you accept? The giver may be wealthy or from a wealthy company, and you might not agree to do anything in return. Still, accepting a substantial gift when there *is* a prospect of further business is likely to evoke a rational expectation of favoritism. If so, then accepting it as simply an expression of goodwill misleads the giver. The giver may think there is a bribe even if the receiver is uninfluenced.

Furthermore, precisely because there *is* a prima facie obligation of gratitude, accepting gifts easily tends to make those who accept them feel obligated to "reciprocate." This tendency is natural in ethical people and may be exploited by gift givers in business. Suppose, however, that we can resist any improper response to accepting a substantial gift. Still, we participate in, and may in fact strengthen, a *system* in which there may be competition to influence business by giving gifts rather than (mainly) by achieving competitive advantage. That system undermines the free market.

Gift Giving Versus Bribery

A gift is something not owed to the recipient and given without a *quid pro quo* (an assurance or indication of something in return): if there is a mutual understanding that something must be done in return, then what is given is not a gift. If what is given in return for what appears to be a gift is mutually expected favoritism in a business decision that ought to have a sound economic basis in a system of fair competition, then the "gift" is very likely a bribe.

Can we always tell whether in accepting something as a gift we are viewed by the giver as taking a bribe? This is doubtful. We may think we can, but others' intentions are sometimes difficult to discern, especially when neither party makes any statement of expected reciprocation. Moreover, the acceptance of significant (non-ceremonial, moderately to highly valuable) gifts in business is fertile ground for self-deception. When the time comes to make a decision about the giver or the giver's company, the memory of the "gift" may exercise an influence on the recipient, even if only subconsciously. If it does exercise a favorable influence, we may have a case of what might be called a *silent bribe*.

Bribery of the clearest kind has now been implicitly characterized: to bribe someone with respect to a future decision is (roughly) to provide something the person considers desirable with the result—call it *uptake*—that the person makes (or intends to make) a favorable decision on the basis of receiving it, usually a decision that would not have been made under the standards that should govern the decision. Five categories should be described here.

1. *Attempted bribery.* This term is most natural where someone offers a would-be bribe, say a payment, that is rejected.

Attempted bribery may also occur where the attempt is to effect a silent bribe, say by giving a "gift" with the unstated expectation of favoritism later. If the gift is either rejected or mistakenly accepted simply *as* a gift, the attempted bribery fails.

2. *Aborted bribery.* Some people who accept something valuable intended to influence them are said to have "accepted a bribe" even before they can act on it. It can be true that they have accepted a bribe even if they never act on it, either because they back out or because something (such as a bankruptcy) prevents the favorable action. These cases, in which a would-be bribe is accepted but not acted on, are aborted bribery. On the offerer's side, both these and rejected bribery offers are related to successful bribery somewhat as attempted murder is related to actual murder. Trying to do a wrong is itself a wrong. On the recipient's side, a rejected bribery attempt may be virtuous (though rejection may also be a ploy to get a higher offer), but aborted bribery shows a reprehensible willingness to do wrong.

3. *Ineffectual bribery.* Third, on the recipient's side, a bribe may occur even if the recipient already intends to do the deed and adopts no new aim as a result of the bribe. Call this an *ineffectual bribe* (though it may have the "internal" effect of strengthening the motivation to do the intended deed). Accepting something meant as a bribe need not change one's decisions, but because of the *willingness* it shows to subvert the decision process, it reveals a kind of uptake and is still wrong. Thus, accepting it would still be wrong even if one later decided *not* to do the deed. Another kind of ineffectual bribe—a kind of "*misappropriated*" *bribe*—may resemble a case in which a thug paid to rob someone decides to rob the payer instead. The would-be briber fails to get the recipient to do the desired thing, and that person commits the double wrong of defrauding the former by appearing to take the bribe and then making off with the payment.

4. *Conditional bribes.* Fourth, bribery is possible even when the recipient does not intend the requested action, but will do the deed if necessary. Consider a person who knows the

company will probably give a contract to a certain bidder. The person may still take a bribe from the bidder with the announced intention of pushing the deal through *if* conditions require a push. As it is, the prediction is borne out and the person simply votes with the majority without pushing. The bribe is thus not "needed," but it is not ineffectual since it does produce the plan to act *if* necessary. But what if the deal is good and should go through, and the recipient of the bribe is aware of this? Does this knowledge excuse accepting the bribe? The recipient still fulfills the conditions of bribery by making the required plan, and taking the bribe is still wrong. It is a major point of ethics that one can do the right thing for the wrong reason. The bribed voter is compromised and deserves at most partial credit for voting for the right plan. This behavior clearly illustrates a failure of integrity.[64]

5. *Bribes as material items.* "A bribe" can be a material thing given, as opposed to the acts of giving or offering it described above. Bribery in either the behavioral or even the material sense cannot be defined, however, in terms of monetary or any material value, and the value of what is given—of *a* bribe—need not be great. Some people's price is low. Some overrate what is given (phony "Swiss watches" with prestigious names are one example). It is common, of course, for those who take bribes to set a price as high as they think they can get for the desired act.

It has been said that there are places where one simply cannot get contracts without paying a bribe. If so, could one argue that the case is like that of child labor when the alternative is worse? Some would, but every case is different and there is no fully comparable argument because, in child labor, there need be nothing *intrinsically* bad (as opposed to potentially bad because of the vulnerability of children). There is, however, one analogy: in both cases, the system that presents the problem should be changed and *can* be changed only with the cooperation of virtually all parties significantly involved. This kind of need for systemic reform will be considered in the next chapter.

13

NATIONALITY, INTERNATIONAL BUSINESS ETHICS, AND COSMOPOLITANISM

The rise of the Internet and improvements in transportation have underlined the point that the world is getting smaller. It is also getting more interconnected. Many people communicate regularly with others abroad, international travel is increasingly common, and (especially in Europe) national boundaries no longer constitute the barriers they once were. International trade in a largely free market has increased competition in many products, such as electronics and clothing. In some countries, including the United States, international competition has caused some nationalistic resentment. Some of this is due to outsourcing.

Outsourcing

Suppose you manufacture furniture in the United States. Your machines are expensive and skilled workers are scarce. You lose your best worker in the department that makes wooden legs and spindles for chairs. These are made from a different kind of wood than the seats, and you have had to process them differently. You find that a company in another part of the country can produce these parts for you more economically. If you stop making them and buy them from that company, you will have *outsourced* this part of your product. If this did not sometimes require layoffs or terminations, fewer people would object. Suppose, however, that you need not lay anyone off. Then, although you may deprive some of your workers of the sense that together they make the whole chair, this could be a tolerable cost. They might still have the sense of meaningful work that goes with contributing to a lasting and beautiful product.

The story continues. Imagine that you have had to import certain woods. You discover that you can make whole items, such as benches, from them in a country closer to the wood's source. You might then outsource those items as a whole—"offshoring" them in this case, since the company producing them is foreign—but you can still put your name on the product. (You might still do the finishing, which is important and is distinctive of your domestic factory.) But you might also decide to open your own factory, say in Vietnam. Since the work previously done in the United States is now done there, some may describe you as shipping "American jobs" abroad. Is this a fair description? Have you had to fire or lay off any employees? If so, you might have instituted a retraining program, continued their insurance for a time, and given generous severance pay. They might also have found equally good jobs in any case.

Let us suppose, however, that in building the factory you are actually expanding your business and that the comparison you make in deciding to outsource is with making the products domestically. Must there be someone near you or in another part of the United States who would have gotten your orders if you had instead expanded your present factory or opened a factory elsewhere in the country? Suppose not. Domestic expansion might then not be profitable, even if it would have provided more jobs domestically. Moreover, even for your overseas factory you might hire some managers domestically, so at least those new jobs are created. You might also create some new domestic sales jobs to market your new products. Another factor is competition. Even apart from expansion, you might lose money if you do *not* do some manufacturing abroad where labor is much less costly. You might then have to lay off some workers.

These examples show that the economic impact of outsourcing is difficult to calculate. It cannot be automatically assumed that jobs are eliminated in the area of the manufacturing business in question or even that the total number of jobs in that sector is reduced in the long run. But let us take an ethical perspective. From the point of view of beneficence, and certainly from a utilitarian point of view (which makes universal beneficence ethically central), the total good one does is a standard of conduct. Might you not do a great deal of good by opening a factory in a country where it provides jobs for people who either have none or vacate less attractive jobs to take your offer, thereby making room for others less well off? And might you not be a good, even exemplary, employer there, perhaps seeding reforms in the laws and practices governing business?

It is not only a utilitarian point of view that can support certain kinds of outsourcing. Like utilitarianism, the common-sense ethical framework that has guided this book treats all persons as meriting concern. Indeed, many ethical perspectives (though not classical utilitarianism) treat the reduction of suffering—which is often achievable by improving working conditions—as more important (other things equal) than the positive increase in happiness. It is true that ethics allows us to give some special weight to relationships with people close to us and to our countries.[65] But ethics does not allow us to take any human beings as valueless or even unworthy of assistance, and the possibility of contributing to life in other countries can sometimes offset the competing considerations that favor a more nationalistic orientation in business.

Cultural Adaptation, Relativity, and Standards of Negotiation

Now consider establishing your factory abroad. You must buy or rent space, hire contractors, managers, and "rank-and-file" workers, and establish operating rules. This will require negotiation, and the rules for that, as well as for day-to-day work, may differ dramatically from those of one's own country. Should our ethics be altered to accommodate the differences in ethos and perhaps in laws too?

General ethical standards are universal, but their applications in a given setting may vary with culture. It is unethical, for instance, to treat people disrespectfully; but in one culture it may not be disrespectful to yell at a slow yet able factory worker, whereas in another it would show disrespect. The universal principle expressing an obligation of respectfulness *applies* in both situations, but is *violated* in only one. This principle applies differently *relative* to different cultures. When in Rome, we may sometimes do as the Romans do. Indeed, the same example bears on a single culture at different levels: in the United States a supervisor of factory workers who has known them for many years may yell at them without offending, but rarely if ever could a CEO yell at other executives without implying disrespect.

These cultural differences might or might not be provided for in an ethics code. To be sure, a given company with very different categories of employees and tasks could have two or more code provisions that overlap but are quite different overall. Each code might require treating all employees with respect (hence overlap), but one code might specifically tolerate yelling on some occasions, say on a noisy factory floor, and the other might not.

There is a general point here. A code should not attempt to list every specific kind of behavior to which it applies. Ethics presupposes that we are *autonomous*—roughly, self-governing—and that we can sensitively regulate our conduct by sound standards. A code should be readily applicable and should be worded to make its proper applications clear for those who understand and accept it. It should also be role-modeled by a company's leaders.

In international business, as in business anywhere, negotiation is crucial for success. People with a common interest must discuss their options and arrive at a decision. This often requires compromise, sometimes with the result that at least one party is less than fully satisfied. But a fair compromise may be accepted as such on both sides (or all sides if there are more than two) and leave all concerned happy. You may pay more than you wanted to for a factory site; but I, as a native of the country in question, may do more than you expected to help you find a good construction company and obtain building permits.

Must ethical negotiation require seeking the satisfaction of all parties? This holds in ideal cases, but to require it would go too far. Some kinds of satisfaction may sometimes be clearly unattainable or unreasonable. Someone selling a family farm may be unhappy even with a very good price and a promise to save trees. We can say, however, that ethical standards, including obligations of respectfulness, always *apply* to negotiation. In practice, this implies fairness in the terms proposed (a dimension of justice), an effort to maximize satisfaction on both sides, and respectfulness in the manner of negotiating.

Ethical Limits in Negotiation Strategies

Negotiations should be honest, but there are negotiation settings (and perhaps cultures or subcultures) in which honesty is not expected. Given that the obligation of veracity is not absolute, might we say that here it is overridden by the force of local custom? I think not. But the issue is not simple. Consider lawyers speaking for their clients. If it is understood that they are taking the client's point of view and relying on information supplied by the client, they are not necessarily lying in saying something false (even if they suspect it is false). For one thing, there need be no intent to deceive, but only an effort to make a good case. Businesses also have negotiators who are understood to be speaking from a point view rather than for themselves. They are advocates making a case for their clients.

Consider a corporate negotiator who has a budget of $5,000,000 to get a contract to build a small factory. The negotiator may be told that $1,000,000 for the land is maximal, but also that the Board might authorize more if necessary. If offered a price ten percent higher, might the negotiator say "I can't pay that" without lying? (The "can't" is indefinite in meaning.) The statement is not believed to be true by the negotiator but need not be analyzed and also may not be definitely believed false by the negotiator. Moreover, the hearer is understood to take this as a move in negotiation, not as a statement of conviction. This needs emphasis because the obligation not to lie is grounded in part on the tendency of lies to produce false beliefs, and in a negotiation context one is often likely *not* to be believed.

It would be different if one were sole owner of a company and falsely said "I do not have that much money." If I know this is flatly false, I should not seriously assert it. Suppose, however, that it is literally true but, in saying it, I am concealing that I can readily *borrow* to obtain that much. This kind of withholding of information is not lying (and might not deceive, since the other party may know my high credit rating). A good negotiator on the other side would see that it is incomplete information. It would still be a potentially misleading statement, however, and we must face the question whether ethical negotiation can be misleading in certain ways.

Let us approach an answer by degrees. Negotiation must not be *fraudulent*, embodying lies or misrepresentations of a similar kind. It also must not be *exploitive*, where this is taking unfair advantage of the other party. Suppose, for instance, that I lend someone money, with the loan secured by land. After getting a geologist's report indicating the likely presence of oil on that land, I foreclose on the loan though I do not need the money and know that if I extend credit for another month (at fair or even higher interest), the party could pay the debt (and might even realize that the region is believed to have oil). This kind of opportunistic foreclosure is likely to be legal in most countries, but in most cases would be unethical.

The Relation Between Ethics and Law

This example is a good one to show that not everything unethical *should* be illegal,[66] whether by national or international statutes. If I have to borrow money and secure it with land, I should size up the lender and assess my risk. The lender takes a risk, too (unless the land has far more value than the loan, in which case I should resist pledging its entire value). Should we have laws that prohibit foreclosures where there has been a change in value of what is pledged that favors the lender? This would entangle government in business in an undesirable way; it would increase the number of lawsuits; and it would decrease lenders' willingness to give credit (since recovery of funds upon default would be more difficult), thereby hampering business. Fraud should be prevented by law, but it is ethics we must rely upon to prevent the greedy from taking unfair advantage of anomalies in a system that is free and not intrinsically unfair.

The rejection of fraud and exploitation in business does not rule out negotiation and other business practices that are *shrewd*. Shrewd but honest negotiators may skillfully represent the facts favorably to their point of view and may mislead all but other shrewd negotiators. They may also succeed without being exploitive. It is desirable to have laws that *procedurally* support fair negotiations, say by providing for access to information about taxes and utilities to facilitate real estate assessment, about penalties levied against a business being assessed for credit, and about economic conditions in a community being evaluated as a factory site. Legal penalties for fraud and breech of contract are also needed. But a free democracy should not dictate the exact conditions for fairness in negotiation. The same holds for international bodies that do (or someday will) oversee international business and may have legal authority in their own right.

To be sure, when we lose out to a shrewd negotiator, we may *feel* exploited, but getting less than we might does not imply being *cheated*. Ethics does not require giving up the attempt to maximize one's interests in negotiation, but it also does not license taking unfair advantage of others. This applies even where one is in a country whose laws or customs permit exploitation.

Although there is no formula for determining when a negotiator goes beyond shrewdness to exploitation, we can gain clarity by considering how *bluffing* may fit into this picture. If bluffing entailed lying, there would be less need to single it out, and some kinds would be illegal or a basis for a reasonable lawsuit. But, as in poker, bluffing need not entail lying. If I tell you I cannot afford to sell for less than $1,100,000, I may be bluffing without lying, because the term "cannot afford" is vague enough to cover the case in which I must borrow if I receive less and will also be criticized by my employer, yet I do intend to sell to you for significantly less if I have to. Suppose you say, "The deal doesn't make sense for me at that price; I'll have to look at other properties, but you can call me within three days if you can meet my price." You need not be lying because you do not say when you will look at other properties and you will do so if our negotiations fail; in any case, you are ready to pay my price or one close to it if you have to. In many cases, there is another reason neither of us is lying: it may be that the *understanding* of negotiation in our situation suspends the normal presupposition that people believe exactly what they assert.

By way of balance, we should remember that ethical business requires not only good general ethics, but *strategic prudence*. A negotiator lacking either one is deficient. Both, moreover, require sensitivity to differences in culture and context. When bluffing involves no lying and simply gives a misleading appearance to someone lacking acuity or—more likely—causes uncertainty that may produce concessions, it may be part of ethical negotiation. But a willingness to bluff easily leads to lying, and bluffing, as potentially exploitive, is an undesirable element in business practice and is commonly counterproductive.

Intellectual Property, Technology Transfer, and Porous Borders

Confidentiality and trade secrets have come up, but we have not yet considered the difficult overlapping topics of intellectual property and technology transfer. If you write a book on management or a computer program designed to facilitate inventory control, you have an intellectual property. If you have plans for building a nuclear power plant, you have both an intellectual property and, potentially, an important technology. Even making furniture implies using a technology, and when a company institutes a technology elsewhere we may speak of "technology transfer." There is a technology for efficient shaping and finishing of furniture parts; there is a much more complicated technology for building a nuclear power plant; and as we know from controversies about Iran and North Korea, because the technologies and raw materials for operating nuclear power plants can be used to build nuclear weapons, technology transfer raises issues in international business ethics.

The nuclear power plant problem is addressed by international law, but enforcement in the international arena is difficult, and the safety of the environment and indeed the peace of the world may depend on voluntary ethical conduct by companies having potentially dangerous technologies. In recent years, a Pakistani scientist was charged with illegally conveying crucial nuclear technological information to Iran. This is a kind of case in which business ethics also figures. The technology was likely developed through work done under contract with a company (or governmental employer) having a claim to control its intellectual property and technological secrets. Dissemination of intellectual property or technological information developed by or for a company without permission from that company is a breech of confidence and, more generally, a failure to fulfill a promissory obligation.

Suppose, however, that you are the author of an original book or the creator of a technology. You may give permission for the use of the ideas or information. To whom should you give it and at what price? As to price, the only comment needed here is that it should be fair, as opposed to price gouging by the seller or exploitation by the buyer. Suppose you create a vaccine that prevents "bird flu," and an epidemic threatens. You are entitled to a healthy price, as where giving the vaccine to appropriate drug companies would make you wealthy yet leave it affordable under normal medical budgets. But one should avoid exploiting people's vulnerability by requiring them to go deep into their life savings for the needed dose.

The case is somewhat like that of an individual's owning the only water supply that, in wartime, is not poisoned. Even if government would allow it—and here even free market theorists would likely make an exception to the usual sanctity of private property and agree to temporary governmental requisition—one should not withhold it from all who cannot pay a huge price. Here again ethics allows a good profit, but not exploitation. Nonetheless, there is no good simple formula for ethical price determination. Government may set limits depending on people's needs; but if government does not overextend its authority and set the limit too low, there will likely be a range in which charging the highest price one can get is greedy, charging a generous intermediate one is beneficent, and charging a still lower one is supererogatory. A virtue ethicist might call the second case a mean between excess and deficiency.

Ethics and Law in International Business

Some of the important issues in international business ethics concern both ethics and law and their relation. Suppose your company sells munitions and reloading kits for common kinds of small arms—kinds usable against innocent people by a tyrannical government or by terrorists. Suppose, too, that because of a loophole—or a delay in passing restrictive laws—you can legally sell the kits to agents of oppressors. This is the kind of case in which ethics requires more self-control than law mandates. One should not sell to such people. What is perfectly legal may be unethical.

A harder question is whether you may sell or give the munitions or a technology for reloading to a group you know to be defending the innocent, where this technology transfer is *illegal* in the country in question. The answer depends on more variables than can be tracked here. If the country is a brutal dictatorship practicing genocide, the answer may be positive. What is illegal may be ethical. The larger issue suggested by such cases is what constitutes a desirable set of international standards for business in these and other difficult matters. Some of these standards are articulated in documents written by the United Nations (UN) and other non-governmental agencies, and discussing them is not possible here. We can, however, see one procedural point: this kind of problem should be addressed by international bodies as well as by companies concerned with protecting or promoting justice.

Another difficult question concerns a kind of case we have already encountered: how to assess tradeoffs between good and bad effects of international business. During 2005 and 2006 there was controversy about compromises made by U.S. Internet companies (notably Google and Yahoo) in order to provide service in China. The Chinese government required information about users as a condition for operating, and there was evidence that at least one critic of the regime was unjustly imprisoned as a result of information supplied by Google. The details are too complex to describe here, but some of the ethical issues are clear. On the one hand, an Internet company should not be complicit in human rights violations. On the other hand, opening the Chinese market to a wealth of information as was done might well support political and human rights reform over time.

Where censorship is imposed by a government, ingenious Internet users may often be expected to penetrate the censorship barriers. How much censorship, if any, should an Internet company (or any media company) agree to, assuming one may expect the overall effect of these businesses on human rights to be positive? And if you agree to any access by government to communications over your lines, should you not prominently inform your users of this? This is crucial—though in some countries government access would be assumed in any case. Government surveillance is typically a threat to liberty, and the threat is greater where the surveillance is unknown to those subject to it.

Many other factors go into evaluating the tradeoff between supporting liberty by making contributions in communication or technology and, on the other hand, working with an oppressive regime. It can be very difficult to tell when that tradeoffs might be favorable to doing business in a given country. Whatever its decision, a company should oppose the policies that restrict freedom of information. This may not succeed if only one or two companies do it, but focused and collective international pressure is a powerful force. To seek support for reforms is a responsibility of ethical business; to yield to repressive rules without protest is complicity.

International Cooperation and Cosmopolitanism

The ethical questions raised by technology transfer and intellectual property resemble some of those concerning bribery. Above all, even if some nations have laws and practices that address these problems, without international cooperation ethical companies may suffer. Your competitors from another country may pay a bribe and get a contract even if you will not take a bribe. To make matters worse, they may not do as good a job—say with a public works project like a dam—to the detriment of the population.

Suppose, however, that there is an international consortium with the power to levy fines or at least to investigate and bring collective pressures on companies that violate reasonable standards. The Caux Round Table Principles and the United Nations Global

Compact are examples of such organizations, each of which has much international support. A related effort is the Global Reporting Initiative, under which companies are asked to report annually on ethically relevant economic, environmental, and cultural aspects of their performance.[67]

The Caux principles include a number that recognize the legitimate claims of all groups affected. Their concern ranges from corporate contributions, to "justice and world community," to going "[b]eyond trade friction toward cooperation," to "[s]upport for multilateral trade," to respect for the environment. The document is partly based on the idea that public information on the performance of businesses—a kind of *international transparency*—supports ethical business. Collective pressure from peers, such as the companies in the Global Compact, may also support it and may indeed result in national or international legislation to enable enforcement where voluntary compliance is absent.

International groups have limited power without the support of governments. It is the latter that pass laws backed by fines and prison terms. There is, to be sure, a World Court, and some nations respect its verdicts. But some countries (including the United States) have declined to allow the Court to try their citizens even for crimes in other countries. *Nationalism*—a kind of favoritism toward one's own country's interests over those of other countries or of humanity as a whole—remains a powerful force in the world.

Granted, it is no longer acceptable in international relations for one nation to say that it is "better" than others, but the egalitarian ideas of the U.N. Declaration of Human Rights—which treats all people as having the same basic rights—do not in actuality govern international conduct. The Declaration affirms, for instance, rights to life, fairness (in compensation as well as other dealings), freedom of conscience, privacy, free expression, private property, and due process. Affirming these rights is implicit in the ethical principles stressed in Chapter 4. Defending those principles and these rights does not imply that nations must treat citizens of other countries equally with their own in all matters, but the standards of ethics do require more consideration of other nations than most nations now exhibit.

Contrasting with nationalism is *cosmopolitanism*. In a strong form, this is the view that everyone should be under the same "international" government. This is not proposed here; the point is only that movement away from nationalism and in the direction of *limited* world government may be needed if sound business ethics is to be internationally realized. Nuclear technology has been mentioned. There are already international agreements concerning non-proliferation of nuclear weapons, but no international agency can enforce them without the concurrence of at least the governments represented on the U.N. Security Council. The same holds for technology transfer and global warming. Given the disparity between long-range demand for fossil fuels and their supply, development of certain automotive technologies is ethically obligatory and promotion of wasteful ones is ethically objectionable. But so far, apart from market pressures, nations may do largely as they please in this matter.

To be sure, the more ethical companies are, the less need there is for regulation. But we know too much about human psychology to expect that good ethics will make legal regulation unnecessary. The world has become much smaller as a result of the Internet and global business. International business ethics is essential for global justice, international peace, and the prosperity of the world's growing population. International cooperation and, in some cases, international laws with teeth are needed to ensure success.

14

CONCLUSION

We have considered business ethics in three broad areas: its place in a free democracy, its guiding role in the management of companies, and its function as a set of regulative standards for international business. Business ethics reflects a certain tension that derives from the different and sometimes competing thrusts of ethical standards themselves. This tension is also reflected in the foundations of democracy. On one side are liberty and the rights that go with it; on the other side is equality among persons, with the restrictions on extreme liberty that it imposes. Business ethics must provide standards that safeguard economic freedom—including free competition—while also protecting the vulnerable from its exercise in exploitive ways.

In a well-founded constitutional democracy, law serves this balancing function to a significant degree. But just laws must ultimately derive from ethical standards as understood in a democratic framework, and even just laws cannot provide all the standards needed for ethical business. Law is coercive in a way ethics is not, and if all our ethical obligations were enforced by law, our liberty would be drastically reduced. In reality, these ethical obligations are often matters of judgment that cannot be codified to the extent required for legislation and legal enforcement. Even if they could be codified, ethics *asks* of us more than the minimum it *requires* of us. Seeking to avoid criticism for being unethical, as where we violate no one's rights and live within our own, is simply not sufficient for meriting ethical approval. Ethical businesses should aim at higher standards. They should aim at making possible a high quality of life for those they employ and should contribute to the quality of life in the societies in which they operate.

In the larger society in which businesses operate, then, they should do more than anyone has a right to claim from them. Their constituencies are not just their owners and employees. To do no beneficent deeds beyond those demandable as someone else's entitlements is an ethical failure and normally deserves criticism. There is no formula for determining just how much businesses should do for their constituencies. This is a matter of judgment and should be considered in the light of the reflective desires of stockholders and not just of management. There may be companies that will do only as much as is required by law or is essential to maintain their reputation. But a business may want to do far more. If the virtue of generosity is a guiding standard, businesses will do some deeds that are supererogatory. These can take us beyond earning approval to meriting praise. That high status has generally been considered economically valuable. Let us hope that good ethics always is "good business," but profit should not be the only motivation to be ethical.

The common slogan "good ethics is good business" has not been discussed in previous chapters. There are two reasons. First, the main concern of this book is to describe and promote what *constitutes* good ethics in business and to help in achieving better decisions in business practice. Second, it may be assumed that— at least for those who are not unethical—there are reasons to be ethical even if ethical conduct does not contribute to profits. It might be added, however, that there is reason to believe—as many successful businesspeople do—that doing business ethically *does* contribute to profits in the long run. Just how much it contributes depends on the society in question and the specific context in which a business operates. It would be good if the profit motive could be more often enlisted in the service of ethics, but it would be a sad day for humanity if this were the only motive supporting ethics in business. It surely is not.

Business ethics has many special standards. We have applied a number of them to specific topics, such as marketing, affirmative action, compensation, privacy, gifts, negotiation, and international relations. This book proposes a set of anchoring principles to provide a decision framework for ethical business. These affirm obligations of justice and non-injury, of liberty and respectfulness, of veracity and fidelity, of beneficence and self-improvement, and of reparation and gratitude. These principles cannot be placed in a rigid hierarchy—no one is more important that any other in *every* possible case—and they apply differently in different contexts. But their *relevance* in ethical decisions is universal, and their *valence*—their thrust for or against certain kinds of actions—is always positive or negative.

The principles we have explored provide a moral map for navigating the world, though they identify only the major routes. The bearing of these principles on a decision problem is sometimes obvious. Where, as is common, it is not, there is no substitute for considering each relevant obligation—and the facts that ground it—and comparing it with any obligations that conflict. A balanced, sound judgment should be sought. Whether we have achieved it can be tested by universalizing. We consider the judgment as precedential in comparable situations, formulate a rule of conduct on the basis of our grounds for making it, and assess that rule.

Some of the basic obligations, such as those calling for honesty, can be prominently placed in a company's code of ethics. Moreover, specific principles that emerge from a company's mission or from its precedent-setting decisions may figure as subsidiary standards. But codes of ethics cannot reasonably cover every case. Codes and mission statements also require discussion and interpretation. Here leadership and the corporate culture it so heavily influences are particularly important. Codes and mission statements should not be mere window dressing, nor even documents sincerely endorsed but left to speak for themselves.

Ethical business needs not just ethical leadership but leadership in ethics. Management should address ethics and should discuss its ethical standards in the context of its decisions. These include personnel decisions as well as determinations of policy. In this regard, some businesses can draw on the ethical support of religious commitments of their employees. This is possible, in limited ways, without compromising the religious neutrality to which many companies are committed. Other businesses may not have neutrality commitments and can, for instance, articulate ideals of the fellowship of all as "created equal" in building teamwork or of religiously enjoined charity in generating support for donations to community projects.

In the international domain, religious differences are among those that must be respected. This ethical obligation goes both with rights of liberty and with respectfulness. But where a religion does not support a moral standard, such as the requirement of justice that entails treating women and men equally, ethical managers may resist its influence and seek reform. There are good and bad ways to do this, however, just as there are good and bad ways to seek reform of a system in which bribery is common practice. Here international cooperation is crucial. One of the challenges of the future is to achieve an international business climate in which globalization will work for the benefit of all and the exploitation of none. The basic knowledge and technological capacity to realize this goal are perhaps in sight, but they will not succeed unless they are guided by ethics.

BRIEF CASE SCENARIOS

〰️

1. *Distribution of profits (Chapters 2, 3, 4, and 8)*. You are on the Board of Directors of a company with 1,000 employees that operates in a small city and has had a good year. This is the first good year in the past five (the others were weak, with no profit). You see two competing options regarding the profits (there are other options, but assume they have been ruled out). (1) You can declare a substantial dividend, which is good for the stockholders (who have had only token dividends during those years, though the stock price has been virtually level in a mainly down market). (2) You can distribute most of the earnings in bonuses to the employees, who have worked very hard to move the company forward. You attribute some of the success of the year to the new CEO and must also provide an increase in her compensation. You have to decide how increasing it fits with option 1 and 2. What strategy would you use to decide between these options and how would you approach an increase for the CEO? (You might speak in terms of percentages of the profit in the distribution or specify hypothetical amounts of money, or both.)

2. *Greasing the wheels (Chapters 5, 12, and 13)*. Consider the following case outline. Your company seeks a contract

with a certain foreign government. It is widely believed in the business community that securing a contract with this government requires paying an official two percent of the contract amount. You discover that this is not a published requirement in that country or elsewhere, and in your preliminary negotiations you are asked by the official who requests the money to keep the payment confidential. Competitors are also prepared to bid the job; you think they would pay the money, and you fear losing a contract that would be profitable. However, your company has a policy against giving bribes. Still, most of its business is domestic, so you wonder not only about exactly what counts as a bribe, but also about whether the prohibition applies to your company's dealings with foreign business. To complicate matters, your belief is that the contract, which is for servicing a power plant, is important for both the daily lives of the people of the country in question and its natural environment. You also believe that your company can do the best job in the relevant engineering tasks, though, from industry gatherings, you know the principals in the other two companies who are in the running for the job and you are sure that those companies can do the job with basic competence. You have the authority to pay out the money, and you have forty-eight hours to make a decision. What might you do and why?

3. *Limitations of advertising (Chapter 6)*. Consider the following case outline, which concerns an important aspect of marketing. You are part of senior management in the marketing division of a company that sells soft drinks. You would like to promote a new line of non-alcoholic beer. To make it fashionable, especially for teens, your advertising team has come up with beachside ads that show a party in which girls are wearing brief bikinis and boys very brief suits. Some of the boys can be seen to be eyeing some of the girls. In addition, to avoid

the suggestion of high calorie content, the thighs and stomachs of some of the girls have been reduced by manipulating digital photography. The scene is eye-catching and suggests the high spirits of a beer party. But the scene is also suggestive in a way you do not like. Your researchers tell you that their evidence indicates that this kind of scene is best for sales, but you would not like your own teenage children to identify with its characters. Your colleagues are divided, and you are the swing vote on whether to run the ad or reject it and send the advertising team back to work. What would you do, and how would you justify it?

4. *Determining merit (Chapter 8).* Suppose you must decide how to divide $20,000 in bonus funds between two men on your team. Their merit, in terms of productivity and effort, is equal, but one is single and the other has three small children at home and a wife who is able to do only part-time work. How might the ethical approach you favor help you decide how to do this or justify your decision after the fact (assuming you make the decision "intuitively")? After answering this, suppose that the married man has done two things you disapprove of: (1) on a business trip, before which you mentioned the company policy of minimizing expenses, he submitted expenses for two breakfasts when the hotel provided adequate continental breakfasts with the room cost. You mentioned this policy to him when signing the approval form, and he said he would not do it again; (2) you also noticed his putting a stack of plain envelopes in his briefcase one evening (and you did not mention it, though normally mailings would not be prepared off premises and envelopes would be addressed by an office printer that stacks them and rolls them out in sets). How might these two factors or the difference in family status, affect either your bonus distribution or your annual evaluation? How would you justify the result under your favored ethical approach?

5. *Affirmative action (Chapters 1, 3, 4, and 8).* Imagine yourself as a contemporary American manager considering hiring a minority person for your team, which presently has 20 percent in the minority category. The applicants include males and females as well as minority candidates and "white males" (a phrase common in specifying a large group in the United States that has not qualified for special consideration under U.S. laws or public policies). Indicate two or three kinds of progressively stronger affirmative action (AA) selection standards that you would consider or think you might be asked to consider by a conscientious person to whom you report. What level of AA, if any, does your ethical position call for? Explain how the position can justify that level. How does your position apply to a white male slightly better then the best AA candidate on all criteria apart from any criteria deriving from considerations of ethnicity or gender? What if you have to choose between a minority male and a white female? Are you satisfied with these decisions as ethically adequate? Why or why not?

6. *Employment policy (Chapters 9, 10, and 11).* As manager of your department in a large company, you must approve non-medical planned absences. An employee comes to you with a request to have half an hour twice each workday for religious observances in a nearby house of worship. The person is a recent convert, which explains why the request was not made at the time of employment. You propose allowing one such absence daily in lieu of the two fifteen-minute coffee breaks already built in. The employee responds that this is not religiously acceptable. You now begin reflecting on what options you have, since the employee is a good one you do not want to lose, and religious reasons for absences are generally accommodated by company policy (which, however, does not dictate how to deal with this special case). A major consideration

you also want to take into account is fairness to other employees. You cannot make the requested exceptions for everyone who might ask, and indeed, the extra half hour each day would reduce the employee's productivity by a significant amount. What are two or three options here? Which seems best, and why? What explanation will you give to someone (such as the vice president you report to) of your action?

7. *Multiple billing (Chapters 7 and 9)*. Suppose you are a financial advisor and, like many professionals, bill certain services by the hour. You have a client with an investment portfolio that contains some thirty items and will require, say, five hours of work for your appraisal and recommendations. Before you can undertake this scheduled work, another client appears with the same kind of need for appraisal and recommendations. You notice that about half of the investments are in stocks held by the first client. This will mean that your work for the two together is likely fewer than eight hours rather than ten. What should be your hourly billing policy here? How would it apply to three or more clients with overlapping investments? What will be its implications for clients who come much later and have *only* common investments that you have already assessed? Compare the ethics of billing for such advice in terms of required hours with billing for it in terms of (1) the magnitude of the job, (2) the level of skill it requires, and (3) how long it would take if done by itself.

8. *Personal relationships in the workplace (Chapters 9 and 11)*. Good ethics in business calls for professional conduct in the workplace, and this entails not just competence in some technical realm or other domain of work, but proper conduct in personal relations with other employees. Particularly in judging any potentially romantic relationships, managers may face questions about whether certain behaviors are consistent with

good professional standards. Suppose you notice that a man who reports to you is spending more time than is professionally required speaking with a woman on the support staff who mainly does typing, document preparation, filing, and Internet searches. On two occasions you notice his leaning over her desk and pointing out details of something to be typed. You do not notice her withdrawing, and in walking by shortly afterwards you see no signs of her being unsettled. Would you say anything to him or to her? If so, what? Suppose now that you find the two having a friendly conversation over what looks like a planned dinner in a nearby restaurant that company people sometimes go to. Looking again in the next few days, you can see what appears to be a romantic relationship developing. One sign of it is more conversation than the workflow requires. Should company policy generally prohibit such relationships or specify that they should in no way be manifested on company premises? Would this be parentalistic interference? Should the policy be different where the employees in question are at different status levels in the company? In the light of how you answer these questions, how would you maintain a company culture that is conducive to mutual support and good fellowship ("*esprit de corps*")?

9. *CEO compensation (Chapters 3, 4, and 8).* Recent years have seen much publicity and many complaints about CEO compensation. The absolute numbers are high (with many CEOs receiving tens of millions annually in total compensation while also having lucrative severance or retirement packages—see Table 1 in Chapter 8). As a member of a board of directors representing shareholders, you are considering candidates for CEO. The two leading ones differ greatly. The front-runner among most of the board members is the CEO of a smaller company that has prospered under him. Indeed, he is credited with "turning it around," since

it had been losing and is now solidly profitable. The other strong candidate is a senior vice president in your own company who has shown leadership in many instances, but has possessed limited authority under the retiring strong CEO, who made most of the crucial decisions alone. Suppose you believe that the facts about both do not enable a confident prediction of their success. You are inclined to believe that there is a better than even chance of success on the part of the frontrunner and about a 50–50 chance of success for the insider. You have only slight confidence in this prediction, however, and wonder whether it simply reflects the influence of the reputation of the CEO, but you are confident that neither would be a *poor* leader. An additional factor is this—the cost of appointing the CEO would likely be approximately $5 million per year in salary and bonus and $2–4 million in stock options, with a retirement package valued at $50 million and a (preretirement) severance arrangement that could cost $25 million. The cost of appointing the insider would be approximately half that. The difference is, to be sure, only about two percent of the current company profits, but you still do not find the choice easy. What variables are crucial in your decision? In either case, how might the employment contract be structured to maximize benefit to the company, e.g. in terms of the conditions that must be satisfied for a given value in stock options? In light of these matters, what is the likely best choice, and why?

10. *Fair competition and retail juggernauts (Chapters 2 and 3)*. Fair competition between businesses that supply much the same goods or services is usually conceived in terms of honest efforts by each business to equal or outdo the other(s). Fair competition allows all to advertise, to offer more goods or services than competitors, to find unique ways to deliver services,

to be more enjoyable to do business with, to have more favorable prices, and more. Unfair competition includes sabotaging competitors' supply line or delivery efforts, spreading detrimental rumors about them, and bribing their employees to slow their work pace. These points are not controversial in business ethics. But here the question is whether unfair competition—in a sense implying unethical business—extends to selling below one's cost with the idea of putting competitors out of business before one's losses mount too high (something a company like Wal-Mart might be thought to have done). Suppose one succeeds and then has a local monopoly. Why must this be bad? One still need not take advantage of this and raise prices higher than they would have been in the original market (there would be plenty of profit simply in being the only supplier in the area). It might also be said that there are laws to prevent such monopolistic behavior. But the matter may be even more complicated. If, by cost-cutting of this kind or simply by low pricing, a company dominates a local area, it is unlikely to be the *only* supplier of the relevant goods and services in the region. This will tend to limit its monopoly powers: too high a price for fridges, for instance, and people will find an alternative by driving further or ordering from far away. Here, then, are two ethical questions. First, is pricing below one's cost with a view to putting competitors out of business ethical provided that one does not intend, if successful, to raise prices to the level of "gouging" possible given a resulting monopoly? Second, do consumers or government regulators who see such an underselling practice arising and do not want higher prices after it succeeds have any obligation to resist, and, if so, how should they resist?

11. *Conflict of interest (Chapters 3, 4, and 11).* Suppose you are on the board of directors of a power company

that supplies much of your city. As a prominent businessperson with high community involvement, you are elected to city government. One of your city council duties will be to negotiate with the power company regarding rates and services. Representing the city, you would seek an optimum combination of low prices and good services. As a board member of the power company, you would seek to maximize profits while rendering adequate service to the city. Must you resign from the board, or is it enough to abstain from voting on issues that concern what terms to propose to the city? If not, is it enough also to withdraw from discussions on the board concerning that subject? Would the answer be different if you simply owned stock in the company, say 5 percent of your investment portfolio? If so, why? If there is a way that one can ethically remain on the board, what should one do as council member when the relationship to the power company arises?

12. *Insider trading (Chapters 3, 7, and 9).* If I am a senior manager in a publicly traded company, I may have inside information about company plans. I might, for instance, know that the company is making a (welcomed) takeover offer of a smaller one. The public announcement of this is almost certain to raise the stock value of the target company. I can thus buy some of those shares before the announcement and realize a great gain "overnight" (this purchase could be done by an agent who does not expose my ownership of the stock). What is ethically wrong with doing this? Does it justify making the practice illegal? How does this differ from a case in which I know that my company's new golf clubs will be a great success and I tell my cousin, who has a sporting goods store, to load up on them when they are first made available? I have given a kind of insider information. Is my

cousin doing insider trading or anything otherwise objectionable?

13. *Business expenses (Chapters 7 and 9).* Suppose you have an expense account that, for business trips, gives you an allotment for your meals, lodging, and transportation. If your dinner allowance is generous enough to cover a friend you would like to see, may you simply claim the allowed amount though only half of it went for your own meal? Compare this with taking a taxi to the airport (which accords with company rules in the circumstances) and inviting a friend who is leaving about the same time to join you. Do your reflections suggest that companies should have detailed rules on such matters? If so, should the policy differ in these two cases? And should such a policy vary in permissiveness with the level of the employee in the company—being more permissive (e.g. allowing for a guest at dinner) with higher level employees? What are some of the issues here?

14. *Child care (Chapters 2 and 9).* What a company offers in child care on its premises or in support for it elsewhere is important, and ethics bears on how much, if any, a business with a strong sense of responsibility to its employees should provide. Ethics also bears on the question whether the role of business in civil society should tend to make it "pro-family." Should companies with, say, 500 or more employees, in a given facility who have one or more children under twelve provide on-site child care? If so, why? If not, should *some* child care be provided, directly or indirectly? Suppose so. This is a cost that indirectly limits services or remuneration to employees who do not use it. Should those using the child care pay something for it, perhaps roughly enough to preserve equity in relation to the compensation of those who do not use it? Finally, consider the possibility that both parents of a child may be employed by the same company and

that it offers employees child care expenses or time off. May it ethically have a policy that limits its support *per "company" child*, rather than per employee?

15. *Elder care (Chapters 1, 3, and 9).* This is an age when people often live long after retirement and, sadly, the body often outlives the mind. One result is that many people must invest time and energy caring for their parents or other older relatives. Should businesses be concerned to support elder care in the same way, or by committing the same resources per employee, as in the case of child care? How does elder care differ from child care in this respect? For instance, should elder care warrant as much time off with pay for emergencies, or as much leave without pay for care that is not provided by the insurance of the elder person(s)? Do salary levels matter in determining how much a company expends to help an employee with elder care? Should employees be eligible for assistance with only one of the two kinds of care or have a budget usable for whichever they choose? What does your position imply about the role of business in society?

16. *Ultrasound and abortion (Chapters 10 and 12).* A recent report says that despite laws in India forbidding doctors from disclosing the sex of fetuses, ultrasound machines have been used to gather this information, and there is evidence of widespread abortions of female fetuses resulting from such information.[68] Suppose you have to decide whether to sell such machines to Indian clinics and that the machines will sometimes be used to identify female fetuses that will then be aborted. What would you decide and why? If your decision might be to sell the machines to licensed clinics, should you impose conditions to prevent such abortions? If so, what conditions, and why would you impose them? Compare this case with one in which a pharmaceutical company must

decide whether to undertake potentially very profit-able research to create a drug that will *pre*select for gender before conception. Assume that this drug would have the good effect of reducing population where its growth is excessive (since many will have fewer children if they can have the sex distribution they want) but will also lead, in many countries, to a larger proportion of male births. What would you decide and why? In both instances, might your deci-sion be properly influenced by religious reasons as well as general ethical reasons?

GLOSSARY

Affirmative action Generically, a policy or activity aimed at advancing the status of a particular group, say women; more specifically and more commonly, an action or policy giving some degree of preference, in hiring, admissions, or other competitions, to a group of people identified by gender, ethnicity, or some other characteristic believed to provide an appropriate basis for preference but not generally considered a qualification for competence in the relevant tasks.

Categorical Imperative *The* Categorical Imperative is Kant's master principle, which he stated in several forms, perhaps most notably as (1) the universalizability principle that we should act only on maxims (principles of action) that we can rationally will to be universal laws, and as (2) the "humanity formula" requiring that we treat persons (ourselves included) never merely as means but always as ends in themselves. *A* categorical imperative is a principle, such as "Keep your promises," that is derivable from *the* Categorical Imperative (There is controversy over whether formulations (1) and (2) are equivalent.)

Conflict of interest A conflict, whether felt or not by the person in question, between two directions in which the person's interests may be advanced, as where one is a member of the boards of directors of two competing companies. Conflicts of interest may or may not be accompanied by conflicting motivation but are generally regarded as something to be avoided when possible.

Cosmopolitanism The view that considerations of the well-being of persons irrespective of nationality take priority in certain matters over national self-interest; strong forms call for international government in such major matters as environmental protection or even in settling regional conflicts, whereas weak versions call for lesser reductions in nations' control over their behavior that affects citizens of other countries.

Cost-benefit analysis   A method of ranking options (such as alternative heathcare plans) on the basis of identifying their possible positive and negative consequences (say their possible impact on the lives of the insured) and the probabilities that those consequences (such as paying for expensive treatments) will actually occur. The net cost or net benefit of an option is found by subtracting the negative values from the positive ones (mathematically, multiplying the probability of each possible consequence of realizing the option by the positive or negative value of that consequence and adding these products). *See also* risk, utilitarianism.

Deontological (duty-based) ethics   An ethical view that affirms at least some ethical duties (obligations or prohibitions) on the basis of the *type* of act in question (such as promise-keeping or killing) as distinct from the consequences of acting, such as the effects (or probable effects) that performing the act will have on human happiness. Kant and Ross are commonly considered deontologists.

Equal opportunity   As applied to a society, a pattern in which all citizens are provided with or at least offered means (such as education) to develop (or "market") their capacities and may enter a fair competition, under publicly ascertainable criteria, for remunerative positions for which they qualify. The term is also applied to similar patterns in companies and institutions.

Ethics   1. In the (presumably central) objective sense, sound standards of right and wrong (e.g. "That company lacks *ethics*; this one exemplifies ethics"); 2. in the disciplinary sense, the *study* of standards of right and wrong (e.g. "a course in *ethics*"); 3. in the personal sense, an *individual's* (or group's) standards of right and wrong, which may or may not match sound standards (e.g. "her ethics should be improved"). Often "morality" is used in senses 1 and 3, as where someone speaks of what is required by morality (by ethics as constituted by sound standards of right and wrong) or of a person's "low" morality (standards of right and wrong lower than the sound ones). *See also* ethos.

Ethos   In a group or company, the *prevailing* standards of acceptable behavior; these may or may not include sound ethical principles (an individual may also be said to have an ethos). *See also* ethics.

Final obligation   *See* prima facie obligation.

Insider trading Buying or selling of (usually) stock by persons with "inside information" on the company or companies involved, as where Enron executives sold the company's stock knowing, on the basis of their executive positions, that it would soon decline.

Intuitionism (in ethics) In rough outline, the view (most famously developed by W. D. Ross) that there is a plurality of basic ethical principles that express prima facie obligations and can be (non-inferentially) known on the basis of an adequate understanding of their content and application. The five-step decision model in Chapter 4 indicates how an intuitionist view applies to ethical problems. *See also* prima facie obligation.

Kantian ethics Ethical views centered on the Categorical Imperative, especially as explicated in Immanuel Kant's *Groundwork of the Metaphysics of Morals* (1785).

Morality *See* ethics.

Negative rights *See* rights.

Parentalism *A* pattern or instance of restricting liberty for the good of the person(s) in question (so called because it is appropriate to parents of small children; it is widely rejected as a mode of governance for adults as citizens in free democracies or participants in free enterprise).

Positive rights *See* rights.

Prima facie obligation (or duty) Roughly, a moral reason for action (such as being a promise keeping) in virtue of which the action will be one's *final* (overall, "all things considered") obligation in the absence of at least equally strong conflicting reason.

Relativism In a common usage, the position that there are no universally valid ethical standards, as opposed to standards rooted in, hence *relative* to, a particular culture or subculture. Relativism is not implied by what might be called *relativizationism*—the view that what one ought to do in a case depends on (and so is relative to) the facts of that case. A relativist would hold that there is no universal prima facie obligation not to kill; a relativizationist that there is, but the obligation may in special cases (such as self-defense) be overridden.

Right (action) In the wide sense, one that is *not wrong*, hence ethically permissible (simply ethical, in one use of that term); in a narrower sense—illustrated by most uses of "*the* right thing to do"—an act that is *obligatory* (thus, its non-performance is wrong).

Rights Justifications against coercion (such as prevention of free speech) or for being given what is promised or otherwise owed to one (such as a salary). The former rights are often called *negative* since they are justifications for *not* being interfered with; the latter are often called *positive* since they constitute justifications for being given something usually considered a good. Rights may be moral or legal depending on whether their justification is moral or legal, and the same conduct may be protected by both kinds of rights.

Risk   The probability (between 0 and 1) of an adverse consequence (of the risky action(s) in question) multiplied by its seriousness, which may be represented by an arbitrary number to indicate how bad the consequence is. Risk is thus a two-dimensional concept such that an almost negligible probability of a very bad consequence may be a low risk, whereas a high probability of a moderately bad consequence may be a high risk; the *total risk* of a policy is the sum of the individual risks of its component risky elements. *See also* cost-benefit analysis.

Slippery slope   A downhill path that, from an ethical point of view, leads from dubious behavior (say regularly letting a supplier pay for one's lunch) to bad behavior (for instance accepting a substantial gift from a supplier) to worse (say taking a bribe to cut out competitors); a slippery slope is usually regarded as a significant temptation to those who embark upon it.

Slippery slope argument   An argument to the effect that since there is a slippery slope between one kind of conduct (such as accepting a gift) and another that is wrong (such as taking a bribe), the former should be disallowed or is wrong, or both.

Stakeholder (of a company)   As most commonly understood, a member of a group having a legitimate interest in a company and to which its management bears some responsibility; stakeholders include owners (notably stockholders), employees (managerial as well others), customers or clients, suppliers, creditors, and persons living in the community in which the company operates.

Supererogatory   Beyond the call of duty, in the sense that the act in question, like giving half of one's resources to charity, is morally good but not an obligation.

Sustainability   For a business activity (indeed any activity), its capacity to be maintained over time at a given level (say, relative to its use of scarce natural resources) functioning roughly at the level in question. The time or level may be left indefinite or may be specified, e.g. in decades or centuries.

Technology transfer   A process in which a technology, such as the applied science needed for building a nuclear reactor, is transferred from a country or company that has it to one that does not (where the recipient country or company is typically less "developed").

Transparency In reference to companies, a measure of how much of what goes on in a company, particularly decision making, can be seen by those who seek information about the company; most often used to designate degree of such information accessible to employees, shareholders, and analysts who assess the business or its stock.

Utilitarianism In the most prominent formulations (e.g., by Bentham and Mill), roughly the view that right acts are those that are at least as good as any available alternative in contributing to the "proportion" of human happiness ("benefits") to human suffering ("costs"). The view is sometimes applied to a smaller population, such as that for which a legislature or corporation is responsible. *See also* cost-benefit analysis and Figure 2, p. 14.

Value (n.) Roughly, the worth of something, either (1) intrinsic worth (also called intrinsic *value*), the worth it has in itself, apart from its consequences, or (2) instrumental worth, its worth as a *means* to something else (on most views, instrumental worth implies that its possessor is ultimately a means to something having intrinsic value). A thing (including ethical conduct) can have both intrinsic and instrumental value. What is valuable is not automatically *valued*. (In reference to a *person's* values, "value" means *roughly* a caring attitude toward the thing(s) in question.) *See also* value (v.).

Value (v.) In ethics, to have a positive, caring attitude toward a person or thing. Valuing normally embodies viewing the person or thing in question as in some way good. Valuing is a psychological notion that stands to the objective (normative) notion of value roughly as belief stands to the true: valuing befits the valuable in the way believing befits the true. What is valued need not actually have value. *See also* value (n.)

Virtue A broadly action-guiding trait of character for which the person merits a kind of praise; it may be intellectual (logicality), moral (justice), or neither (courage).

Virtue ethics In the most general sense, the view (of which Aristotle provides the most influential example) that virtues, as opposed to rules of action, are ethically central and what we ought to do is determined through a proper exercise or understanding of them, as where a just salary increment is determined in the light of what is called for by the exercise of the virtue of justice in the circumstances.

ENDNOTES

1. See John Locke, *An Essay Concerning the True Extent and End of Civil Government,* (1689) Chapter 5, "Of Property."

2. George Sabine, "The Two Democratic Traditions," *Philosophical Review* 61 (1952).

3. See John Rawls, *A Theory of Justice* (Cambridge, MA: Harvard University Press, 1971), for a view of social justice and the foundations of democracy that supports a welfare capitalism. See Robert Nozick, *Anarchy, State and Utopia* (New York: Basic Books, 1974), for a contrasting broadly libertarian, minimalist conception of the just society. Nozick gives property rights a greater role than Rawls and gives welfare—especially through taxation to redistribute income—a much lesser role. For a recent description and critical discussion of Locke's and Rousseau's conceptions of liberty, see Jean Hampton, "The Common Faith of Liberalism," in her *The Intrinsic Worth of Persons* (Cambridge: Cambridge University Press), pp. 151–184.

4. Milton Friedman, *Capitalism and Freedom* (Chicago: University of Chicago Press, 1962), p. 133.

5. See Rawls, op. cit., pp. 14–15. See p. 60 for a formulation nearly equivalent to this one, but note that Rawls later revises the principle (in ways that do not affect our discussion here). See, e.g., pp. 76–83, esp. 83. He also proposes revisions elsewhere in this book and refines his overall view in later works.

6. John Stuart Mill, *Utilitarianism,* Oscar Piest, ed. (New York: Macmillan, 1957), p. 10.

7. The calculative framework used by classical utilitarianiasm is that of a kind of cost-benefit analysis. For an account of this interpretation

(and applications of cost-benefit analysis to other ethical approaches), see my "The Place of Cost-Benefit Analysis in Business and the Professions," *Business and Professional Ethics Journal* 24, 3 (2005), 3–21.

8. The utilitarian standard is different from and does not follow from the *preferential standard* stated in the text. Granted, faced with a choice between A and B where it is clear that A is better one should choose A; but to say this does not support the idea that one should always be trying to *maximize* the good. For critical discussion utilitarianism and questions about the desirability of maximization, see Rawls, op. cit., and Brad Hooker, *Ideal Code, Real World* (Oxford: Oxford University Press, 2000).

9. A detailed account of why utilitarianism should not be understood in terms of the popular "greatest good for the greatest number" formulation is provided in my "Can Utilitarianism Be Distributive: Maximization and Distribution as Standards in Managerial Decisions," *Business Ethics Quarterly* 17, 4 (2007), 593–611.

10. The call for limiting government indicated here is made by Ayn Rand and her followers. See, e.g., Edwin A. Locke, "Business Ethics: A Way out of the Morass," *Academy of Management Learning & Education* 5, 3 (2006), 324–332, and my "Objectivity without Egoism: Toward Balance in Business Ethics" (forthcoming in *Academy of Management Learning & Education*), which is a critical response to some Randian views in business ethics.

11. Immanuel Kant, *Groundwork of the Metaphysics of Morals,* trans. Allen Wood (New Haven, CT: Yale University Press, 2002)), sec. 422, p. 38. Kant apparently has *rational* universalizability in mind in this and the other universalizability formulations of the Categorical Imperative. There is a large literature on how to interpret him, but nothing highly controversial about his view will be presupposed here.

12. Kant, op. cit., sec. 429, pp. 46–47.

13. The notions of treating persons as ends and of treating them merely as means can be clarified even independently of Kant's ethical writings. For an indication of how, and for references to literature on Kantian ethics, see ch. 3 of my *The Good in the Right: A Theory of Intuition and Intrinsic Value* (Princeton, NJ: Princeton University Press, 2004).

14. I refer to Aristotle's *Nicomachean Ethics.*

15. Aristotle, *Nicomachean Ethics* 1105b5 ff).

16. Ethical intuitionism is described, connected with other major positions in ethics, and defended in detail in my *The Good in the Right* (cited in n. 13). Further defense is provided by Michael Huemer in *Ethical Intuitionism* (Basingstoke and New York: Palgrave/Macmillan, 2006).

17. This paragraph and the next draw on ch. 1 of my *Moral Value and Human Diversity* (Oxford: Oxford University Press, 2007), and that book contains a wider discussion of pluralist universalism.

18. The difficulty here has been called the *demandingness problem* and also the *beneficence problem.* For discussion see Hooker op. cit. and, for my approach, *The Good in the Right,* esp. ch. 3. It should be added that if virtue ethics calls for *perfection* in character, then it may be extremely demanding, though not in the quantitative way utilitarianism tends to be. Aristotle is arguably a perfectionist; but even if so, he might hold that a *balance* among the unified perfect virtues might prevent any one of them from demanding a higher ethical standard than a good person can meet.

19. Strictly, we can own only what is not identical with us: owner and property must be different things. Hence, if we are not identical with our bodies, we cannot own them. Can we own their parts—even the brain? If by the laws of nature we can't exist without our brains, it would seem we cannot own them. But suppose I own my kidneys. May I ethically sell one? This is a difficult issue for business ethics and is discussed in my "The Morality and Utility of Organ Transplantation," *Utilitas* 8, 2 (1996), 141–158.

20. For discussion of this issue see Amy L. Domini, *Socially Responsible Investing* (Dearborn, MI: Dearborn Trade Publishing, 2001).

21. Here business executives share a problem with legislators: there can be a considerable disparity between interests and desires. Our desires are easier for us and others to know; our interests are often harder to determine but have more power to provide us with reasons for action. With children, it is easy to discount some desires—the child might only get sick from a coveted third chocolate bar. With adults, desires, even "basic" ones, can be manipulated. One way we can justify going against the expressed desires of our constituents—a kind of limited parentalism, to be sure—is to have an account of their "artificial" (say manipulated) origin or their origin in misinformation and excellent reason to believe the constituents in question will be reflectively glad we did not act on their expressed desire. The problem here is highly complex and cannot be pursued further in this book.

22. For a brief comprehensive discussion of the stakeholder approach in business ethics, see Thomas M. Jones, Andrew C. Wicks, and R. Edward Freeman, "Stakeholder Theory: The State of the Art," in Norman E. Bowie, ed., *The Blackwell Guide to Business Ethics* (Oxford: Basil Blackwell, 2002). I do not treat government as a constituent of ethical business, though it can be considered a stakeholder by virtue of its legitimate need

to regulate and tax. One reason is that its function is regulatory and it is in no way a group for whose benefit the business does or should operate. Another is that its interests in business are secondary in a way those of the constituents are not: apart from protecting such groups in civil society—e.g., employees, consumers, and communities—there would be little if any reason for government regulation of business.

23. For critical assessment of some elements in the stakeholder approach, see Kenneth E. Goodpaster, "Business Ethics and Stakeholder Analysis," *Business Ethics Quarterly* (1991).

24. For an indication of the Golden Rule (Do to others what you would have them do to you) in many religious traditions—African as well as Western and Eastern—see Patrick E. Murphy et al., *Ethical Marketing* (Upper Saddle River, NJ: Pearson Prentice-Hall, 2005), p. 36. For detailed analysis regarding Confucianism see Bo Mou, "A Reexamination of the Structure and Content of Confucius' Version of the Golden Rule," *Philosophy East and West* 54, 2 (2004), 218–248.

25. For a detailed study providing a picture of ethical commonalities among world religious, see Brian D. Lepard, *Rethinking Humanitarian Intervention* (College Park, PA: Penn State University Press, 2002).

26. In *The Right and the Good* (Oxford: Oxford University Press, 1930), Ross called the obligations in question ("duties" in his words) prima facie to indicate that, although they have enough weight to require action if unopposed by any other obligation, they can be overridden by stronger, conflicting obligations. Those who make duty central—including Kant as well as Ross—are often called *deontologists,* but this term is not needed in the text. A useful comparison with Ross's book is Bernard Gert's *Common Morality* (Oxford: Oxford University Press, 2000).

27. This somewhat controversial point is defended in my "Ethical Generality and Moral Judgment," in James Dreier, ed., *Contemporary Debates in Ethical Theory* (Oxford: Blackwell, 2006), pp. 285–304.

28. With this point in mind, I have also developed (in ch. 3 of *The Good in the Right*) a Kantian integration of these principles using my understanding of the Categorical Imperative.

29. One may wonder why the sheer fact that an innocent person may die isn't a moral negative *in itself.* The answer, for a pure (hedonistic or "happiness") utilitarianism, is that moral importance *derives* entirely from hedonic importance. Killing is wrong *because* it tends to reduce happiness. Such act-types as killing, lying, and breaking promises are not *intrinsically* wrong, but on the view of many (including many utilitarians) their cost-benefit ratio (their pleasure to pain ratio) is unfavorable. See, e.g., ch. 2 of Mill's *Utilitarianism.*

30. Chapter 2 of my *Moral Value and Human Diversity* distinguishes between inherent and intrinsic value; both are non-instrumental, the former is such that, as with a beautiful landscape, the appropriate *experience* of it has intrinsic value.

31. Although it is odd to speak of an act that kills a person being performed before the person dies, the idea in the text is that, e.g., a land poisoning is in fact a killing when it is done, but is not normally *known* to be such until someone dies, often much later. Suppose, however, that you know someone will camp there and then die within a year, but can do nothing to warn them. Might you then say, reproachfully, "They should be punished; they've killed innocent campers." Some readers may recall that in Shakespeare's *King Lear* a servant who is stabbed but is still fully alive says, "I am slain" (III, vii). Cf. Mercutio's dying words in *Romeo and Juliet* (III, i).

32. Sustainability may be predicated of change as well as of businesses and activities taken at a given level. Thus development itself is said to be potentially sustainable. See *Our Common Future,* the report of the World Commission on Environment and Development (Oxford: Oxford University Press, 1987).

33. A good short discussion of the case of Malden Mills and its principal owner, Aaron Feuerstein, is provided by Joseph DesJardins in *An Introduction to Business Ethics,* 2nd ed. (New York: McGraw-Hill, 2006), pp. 7–8.

34. In "Persuasive Advertising, Autonomy, and the Creation of Desire," *Journal of Business Ethics* 6 (1987), Roger Crisp argues that advertising that undermines autonomy—such as flashing a product name on a movie screen below the threshold of conscious recognition—is wrong. He sometimes goes further than I do here, e.g. in saying that "persuasive advertising does override the autonomy of consumers," but much of his paper is consistent with and develops the kinds of ideas suggested in this chapter.

35. One unflattering portrait is an Agent Provacateur advertisement in the March 12, 2006, *New York Times Magazine,* which pictures a woman astride an inflated artificial fish on the floor and leaning forward with pursed lips to kiss the mouth of a plastic teddy-bear–like animal which she holds in her hands, while just beneath her loins is a phallic-shaped protrusion from the fish. She is clothed only in black stockings, briefs, a brassiere, and long white gloves (pp. 61–62).

36. DesJardins, op. cit., has some detailed discussion of how Enron's accounting fraud was perpetrated. See esp. pp.125–129. A device apparently legal at the time was the "special purpose entity," a company controlled by Enron but enabling it to hide debt by attributing it to such creations of deceptive accounting.

37. For some discussion of how Enron abused the law to hide debt and for detailed discussion of how accounting can misrepresent the value of leases, see Thomas J. Frecka, "Is Intentional Structuring of Lease Contracts to Avoid Capitalization Unethical? An Accounting Ethics Teaching Case," forthcoming in *Journal of Business Ethics.*

38. For extensive discussion of affirmative action and essays pro and con by writers from different disciplines, see A. E. Sadler, ed., *Affirmative Action* (San Diego: Greenhaven Press, 1996).

39. For some details see "Behind the Rush to Add Women to Norway's Boards," *Wall Street Journal,* Dec. 10 (2007), sec. B, pp.1 and 3. The reported aim is to have women represent 40 percent of directors.

40. For discussion of what constitutes merit in business see Robert C. Solomon, *Ethics and Excellence* (Oxford: Oxford University Press, 1992), esp. pp. 238–239, which offers a long list of criteria of merit.

41. The *Wall Street Journal,* the *New York Times,* and other reputable sources have in recent years often carried figures showing executive compensation.

42. The principle here resembles the second of the two cited earlier from Rawls, op. cit. It should be added that there are differences among constituencies, and in some contexts one constituency, e.g., creditors, may have higher priority, in others another, say stockholders.

43. Herb Baum, in *The Transparent Leader* (New York: HarperCollins, 2004) says that in 2002 "I asked the Board if I could forgo a portion of my bonus to give more to the entry-level folks. I didn't want it to go to the executives, who were already making a good amount…I wanted it to go to the people who made the least" (chapter 2).

44. The kind of consent that legitimizes risky treatment of persons must meet other conditions. It must, e.g., be (up to a point) *reversible* (so that a person can withdraw on discovering what is really happening) and *non-exculpatory,* i.e., not freeing those to whom consent is given for harms done *negligently* even if they have been consented to as possible outcomes.

45. For a brief account of the main whistleblowers at Enron and WorldCom, see *Time Magazine,* December 30 (2002).

46. The text refers to what might be called a *slippery slope warning,* a caution to avoid getting started on a path that leads to wrongdoing. The value of such warnings does not imply the soundness of *slippery slope arguments,* roughly arguments to the effect that since there is a *continuum* from x to y with no clear dividing line, as with, perhaps, deception and lying, then if y is wrong, x should not be performed (lest one slide down into y). Consider the continuum between orange and red to see that this kind of argument is invalid.

47. See the article entitled "IBM to Help Pay for Plans to Curb Childhood Obesity" by William M. Bulkeley, *Wall Street Journal* Oct 24 (2007), p. D4.

48. For discussion of codes in business, with a listing of many representative ones, see Patrick E. Murphy, *Eighty Exemplary Ethics Statements* (Notre Dame, IN: University of Notre Dame Press, 1998).

49. Given how well free democracy has been maintained in England, which does not separate church and state (though the Church of England possesses limited political power), we should not take such separation to be strictly necessary for a free democracy. This does not imply that the separation standard is defective, however. It should also be noted how many factors go into how well a democracy flourishes.

50. For discussion of the Constitution's Free Exercise and Nonestablishment Clauses and references to relevant legal literature, see my *Religious Commitment and Secular Reason* (Cambridge: Cambridge University Press, 2000).

51. A general question arising here concerns the obligations of management toward various "stakeholder" groups. These obligations may conflict, and there is no simple formula for balancing them. Only an overall theory of managerial governance can do that. This book addresses only the aspect of management theory that concerns the ethics of policies affecting religion. Religion often involves, but should be distinguished from, *spirituality,* which may occur in non-religious contexts. For extensive discussion see Oliver Williams, ed., *Business, Spirituality, and Religion* (Notre Dame, IN: University of Notre Dame Press, 2003).

52. Mission statements and ethics codes commonly do not address religion in the workplace and often do not have a nondiscrimination statement that includes both the religious and the non-religious. For a listing of many codes and ethics statements and commentary on them, see Murphy, op. cit.

53. Etiquette—which concerns "good manners"—should also be mentioned. Its requirements are not normally backed by ethical standards, but instead are matters of convention, often of a minor kind (nor are standards of etiquette typically part of a culture's ethos). But *some* breeches of etiquette in some situations can be unethical, as where one offensively seats a senior person in a back row where it is plain that peers have reserved seating.

54. On both corporate culture and styles of governance, Kenneth E. Goodpaster's *Conscience and Corporate Culture* (Oxford: Blackwell Publishing, 2007) provides many cases and is informative concerning ethical and policy issues.

55. One CEO who has treated transparency as central for good business is Herb Baum, op. cit. For a short discussion of major issues in corporate governance see the selected readings and commentary, ch. 16 of Joanne B. Ciulla, Clancey Martin, and Robert C. Solomon, eds., *Honest Work* (Oxford: Oxford University Press, 2007).

56. An account of good leadership in business and some short descriptions of some leaders notable for ethics is provided by Gerald F. Cavanagh, *American Business Values: A Global Perspective* (Upper Saddle River, NJ: Pearson Prentice-Hall, 2006), esp. ch. 8.

57. Mike Merrill, *Dare To Lead* (Franklin Lakes, NJ: Career Press, 2004), p. 10.

58. For discussion of transformational vs. transactional leadership and references to relevant literature on it, see Norman E. Bowie and Pat Werhane, *Management Ethics* (Malden, MA: Blackwell, 2005), pp. 141–142. Their book also contains helpful discussions of a number of topics discussed in this volume.

59. There is now an Ethics & Compliance Officer Association (*http://www.theecoa.org*). It is an interesting question whether it is desirable to combine the ethics and compliance missions, given the kinds of differences noted in the text. As stressed in this book, ethics calls for far more than is properly required by law, but of course much that is unethical is also illegal.

60. In "Managing for Organizational Integrity," *Harvard Business Review* (Mar./Apr. 1994), Lynne Sharp Paine provides reasons to think that compliance-based ethics programs are not as effective in strengthening the ethical culture of a company as integrity-based ones (where ethics receives more emphasis than legal compliance). Other supporting data are provided by a book written by a former monk, Kenny Moore, who became Corporate Ombudsman and Human Resources Director at KeySpan (a major energy company in the northeastern United States, now part of National Grid) and the CEO to whom he reported directly. See Robert B. Cattell and Kenny Moore, *The CEO and the Monk: One Company's Journey to Profit and Purpose* (New York: John Wiley & Sons, 2004).

61. See, e.g., Patrick E. Murphy and Georges Enderle, "Managerial Ethical Leadership," *Business Ethics Quarterly* 5, 1 (1995), 117–128.

62. Joel M. Podolney, M. Rakesh Khurana, and Myrna Hill-Popper, *Research in Organizational Behavior* (2005), p. 22.

63. The rule of courtesy here does not require making sounds most people cannot reproduce without training. It is something like this: pronounce foreign names using the sounds in one's own language that yield the nearest approximation to the sound of the name in the language it belongs to. If, for instance, I can utter only English sounds, I cannot

pronounce "Iran" and "Iraq" as do those native in Farsi and Arabic. But English does have the sounds needed for "Eron" and "Erock" (the pronunciations used by most experts on the region, by contrast with the now common "Irran" and "Irrack," which may have arisen through a mistake that was somehow multiplied).

64. Integrity in one form is simply a kind of integration in a person and is compatible with being unethical (say, in a principled way). But often "integrity" is used to mean moral soundness or, sometimes, just honesty as a major element in this. For an account of integrity with discussion of its ethical importance, see Robert Audi and Patrick E. Murphy, "The Many Faces of Integrity," *Business Ethics Quarterly* 16, 1 (2006), 3–21. Hypocrisy goes against all three kinds; it shows a lack of integration between word and deed, exhibits ethically unsound character, and manifests a failure of honesty.

65. For a critical discussion of the ethical importance of patriotism in comparison with cosmopolitan values, see Louis P. Pojman, *Terorism, Human Rights, and the Case for World Government* (Lanham, MD: Rowman and Littlefield, 2006), which defends a cosmopolitan ethics.

66. One might think that the converse does not hold, so that everything that *should* be illegal is unethical. This is not quite so; we need legally enforced *conventions*, such as driving on the right side of the road. Is driving on the left unethical? Not in itself; it is *violating the rules of the road* that is wrong. This is another case in which the relevant ethical standard is universal but its application is contextual. What might be said is that the only *ground* for a restrictive law is ethical—say, to prevent harm or injustice. But not all laws are restrictive: some define conditions for legally enforceable contracts and do not restrict the liberty in the way the criminal law does.

67. The Caux Rountable was founded in 1986 by executives from Europe, the United States, Japan, Lebanon, Thailand, and other nations; the United Nations Global Compact was a result of an international meeting of business leaders called in 1999 by Kofi Annan (then U.N. Secretary General), and the Global Reporting Initiative began in 1997 through a similar international initiative and issued "Sustainability Reporting Guidelines" in 2002. Many of these guidelines are followed voluntarily by multinational companies. For discussion of these see Cavanaugh, op. cit., ch. 9; his appendices contains the first two (357–362).

68. See Peter Wonacott's article, entitled "India's Skewed Sex Ratio Puts GE Sales in Spotlight: Are Ultrasounds Used to Abort Selectively? Two Clinics' Violations," *Wall Street Journal* (April 18, 2007), pp. A1 and A14.

INDEX